RETURN
TO THE CITY

*How to Restore Old Buildings
and Ourselves in America's
Historic Urban Neighborhoods*

Author—Self-portrait.

RETURN TO THE CITY

How to Restore Old Buildings and Ourselves in America's Historic Urban Neighborhoods

RICHARD ERNIE REED

Photographs by the author except where noted

Doubleday & Company, Inc.
GARDEN CITY, NEW YORK
1979

to Marcia and Alicia
who are part of a renewing America

How can we live without our lives?
How do we know it is us without our past?

John Steinbeck

The Grapes of Wrath

Copyright 1939 © 1967 by John Steinbeck.
Reprinted by permission of the Viking Press
and McIntosh & Otis, Inc.

Library of Congress Cataloging in Publication Data
Reed, Richard E
    Return to the city.

      1. Historic buildings—United States—Conservation
and restoration. 2. Buildings—United States—Conservation and restoration. I. Title.
E159.R43   069.53

Library of Congress Catalog Card Number 78–1217

ISBN: 0–385–14042–8

Table of Contents

Acknowledgments   ix

Introduction   xi

PART ONE   1
I Dream of Home   3
To Find Beauty Again   4

PART TWO   11
Where It's Happening   13
A Celebration of Victorians: San Francisco   16
Building the Future from the Past: St. Paul   23
A Historic City Hidden Among High-rises: Chicago   35
You Can Go Home Again: Marshall   44
A City Saved in Spite of Itself: Portland   52
The Quiet Revolution of the Poor: New York City   63
The Nicest City to Come Back to: Savannah   72
Getting a New Lease on Life: Galveston   84

PART THREE   97
The Struggle to Preserve   99
The End of Optimism and the Beginning of Hope   102
How to Come Back to the City—and Stay   105
Is Preservation "Economically Feasible?"   112
How to Organize for Self-Preservation   121
Creating a New Identity   129

How to Assure Design Unity: In a Building, a Community   *138*
How to Gain Control of Your Community   *145*
How to Put New Life into Old Structures   *152*

PART FOUR   *163*

Must Preservation Mean Displacement?   *165*
Looking Beyond Preservation   *171*

PART FIVE   *179*

Getting Started: Whom Can You Call for Help?   *181*
How to Restore a Building   *185*

Acknowledgments

The author wishes to thank the literally hundreds of preservationists and old-house lovers from across the nation who so generously gave of their time and assistance to make this book what it is—a national expression of a genuine grass-roots urban revitalization movement. To Ted Lentz, Ron Flemming, Art Skolnik, Judith Waldhorn, Ted Leonard, Leo Williams, Maurice Forkert, John Collins, Arthur Ziegler, Jr., Everett Ortner, Ahmad Towfiq, Philip St. Georges, Earl Straw, Larry Mullen, Kristina Butuydas, Greg Paxton, Audrey Rhangos, Elisabeth Gould, Eugene Sizek, Peter Brink, and the many more too numerous to mention but appreciated nonetheless; thank you so much for your special, creative roles in the restoring of America. And to Marcia, my wife, a special thanks for her role as my keenest critic and staunchest supporter.

Introduction

There are few frontiers left in America. The golden west has been explored, freewayed, and subdivided; the trackless forests of the north have been turned into two-by-fours for innumerable suburban split-level homes; the swamps and sandy beaches of the south have been sold for retirement villas. And most of the greenery in between has been turned into carefully cropped lawns of endless neighborhoods looking for a quality of life that somehow escapes that ideal version of the advertised American Dream.

But one frontier remains. It is the city, the morning-after depository of all those get-away-from-it-all dreams of America. It is the place most of us left on our landlocked voyage of trying to find something better. We left the city, worn out, shabby, smelling of old ways and hard times. We slipped out of it like one shrugs off an old coat, leaving it to lie in a heap of parking lots and deteriorated Federal- or Victorian-style houses. A secondhand city, hand-me-downs for the less affluent and less fortunate. And the poor, like the left-behind relations they are, clamor for a better suit of clothes, the shining threads that are so well merchandised in the suburbs.

But a curious thing happened in our rush to be rid of the city, our past, the poor remnants of another kind of America. Some of us have discovered that the newness and apartness of suburbia is not necessarily better. Like the emperor's new clothes, the benefits of newly planted housing tracts and shopping centers are somehow transparent and unsubstantial. Our new environment, sans poverty, sans history, sans care, cannot compensate for a certain sense of loneliness, of estrangement, which often seems to bloom in the suburbs and exurbs where new roots do not grow deep.

A Spirit Calls

The city, even in the shabby wilderness it has now become, is calling many of us back. Because this is where the *genius loci* still resides, the spirit of the place. The ancient Romans built monuments to this special supernatural essence of their cities. They knew that the spirit helped a city to flourish as this spirit set its taproot deep into the earth of memories and fertile experiences. People bloomed under this sense of belonging, of being a part of a continuity of life expressed in the place. They came together around the monuments to celebrate in times of success and to mourn in times of failure. But nevertheless, they came together, one community with its gods of history to express and receive the spirit of the place which was exemplified in the deepening roots of the city and of themselves, the *genius loci*.

History is what the city has, the living and irreplaceable memories of people and events, a boiling mixture of diversity, which no suburban developer can duplicate. And in many cities, in spite of a darkening wilderness of poverty and deterioration, this historical identity still stands in the form of homes and churches, commercial buildings and sentimental monuments.

Often, these last remains of our past only survive thanks to the abandonment of many of the city's residents as they fled to the suburbs in the 1950s and 1960s. "Progress" in the form of the new and the plastic came too late to the quiet residential streets and downtowns. And sometimes urban renewal with its bulldozer mentality occurred too little, allowing a street of brownstones to remain instead of being replaced by the asphalt progress of parking lots.

Yet, for most of us, the city is a place to shun, to forget, to instruct children and women to lock car doors when driving through. It has indeed become a wilderness, a lost frontier, the kind of haunted house that sent shivers down our back as we ran by its shuttered windows in our childhood. The sound that scratches behind the doors, a fearful ghost or a spirit of hope; few will stop to discover which.

The New Pioneers

But in spite of what seems like a continuing migration from the cities, a countermigration seems to be beginning. A new kind of American with a new kind of attitude is coming back to the city to clean the dust of disuse and repair the damage of ill-use from many old structures in the city. We could call them urban pioneers, the new settlers in the old territories of the city. A new kind of American who is establishing himself and herself in bare and barren areas of abandoned buildings and is beginning a new ecological and social cycle of regeneration. They are there so that others may follow.

Awakening from the uneasy sleep of decades, many city streets are again echoing with the laughter of children and the pounding of hammers City officials, who may have for years been acting as caretakers of mausoleums instead of as directors of communities, are becoming educated in the three R's of urban awakening; restoration, rehabilitation, and revitalization.

The urban pioneers, like their forebears, have a vision. They have discovered that the smugness of suburbia has been tempered by the statistical facts of crime, drugs, deterioration, pollution, and civic mismanagement which reside in the village mall as well as in city hall. They see

that the freeway, that long umbilical cord between home and office, is beginning to shrivel because of rising prices and lowering supplies of fuel. They see the high battlements surrounding the acre and one half suburban ranchos grow weak under the pressure of increased operating costs, taxes, and school desegregation.

And they look back at the city and see hope in the face of urban hopelessness. They see the aesthetics of the city's genius loci, the refreshing amenities of historical roots, a personal identity, a sense of community, and irreplaceable architecture and craftsmanship. Most of all, the architecture—a home, a spacious, unique sense of place in which one can grow and become whole. This is what causes the urban pioneer to come back home to the city, to restore a home that becomes a part of a restored community and himself.

Dusty Treasures

In the wilderness of the deteriorated, old inner-city neighborhoods stand treasures more precious than rural mansions. Their names are Eastlake, Georgian, Federal, Greek Revival, Victorian Gothic, Queen Anne, and dozens more. They are history, they have personalities like their generations of owners, they are craftsmanship, they are living spaces worth coming back to, worth making a personal commitment to, worth fighting for.

The urban pioneers, like their earlier namesakes, have to struggle and take risks for what they believe in. The wilderness of the city holds promise, but it also holds fear: The young, white, middle-class couple restoring a brownstone in the middle of acres of partially abandoned Brooklyn tenements; the young family in St. Paul investing every penny and ounce of energy to restore a Carpenter's Frenzy farmhouse in the midst of a burned-out, boarded-up neighborhood. The cold, unrelenting reality of politics, building codes, rehabilitation costs, and communication between the essential diversity of the inner-city soon dispel the pleasant euphoria of the siren call of genius loci.

Then, in order to allow the beauty of history and home to survive, clear thinking and practical tools are needed. The urban pioneer, uncomfortable under his apparent strangeness, must not only defend his home but himself. What right does he have to disrupt the slow death of the city? What right has he to show others that a slum is only a state of mind?

He replies, "People say, 'If you're a pioneer, then what is the wilderness: the slums, the poverty?' I say, hell no. The slums, the poverty are fighting the same enemy we are. If you want my opinion, the harsh wilderness in this urban frontier is local politics, bull-dozer development, banks, insurance companies. They're what we have to fight, to convince them that preservation pays, if we're ever to make the city a decent place to live for all of us."

Sorting Out the Future

The city is a mixture of sentiment and conflict, serenity and strife. It is, in fact, what life is all about. We fled to the suburbs in an effort to get beyond the pressure zone of living, a sort of paradise where there is no poverty, no unmet needs, no history, no leaky faucets. Some, the urban pioneers, have found that you can't run away from history, the cities, the realities of life, as you can't run away from yourself.

Who am I? Where am I? What can I become? These are the questions, if we are lucky, that some day we will ask. To many, coming back to the city is a journey back to ourselves, our roots, our needs. We begin to see the little details of houses and people. If we can deal with the problems and the potential of old buildings and old neighborhoods, we may be better able to deal with ourselves. We all are pioneers. We all have a wilderness to explore.

This book will evaluate both the aesthetic issues of back-to-the-city life and the practical issues of accomplishing effective restoration and revitalization of neighborhoods. Is it possible or practical to build a future from our past? Is it possible to save our cities and in the process maybe to save ourselves?

There are some people, the pioneers, who singly or as a community, have been searching for the answers in the neglected streets of our American cities. We will ask them. Maybe they have found a way for some of us who wish to follow.

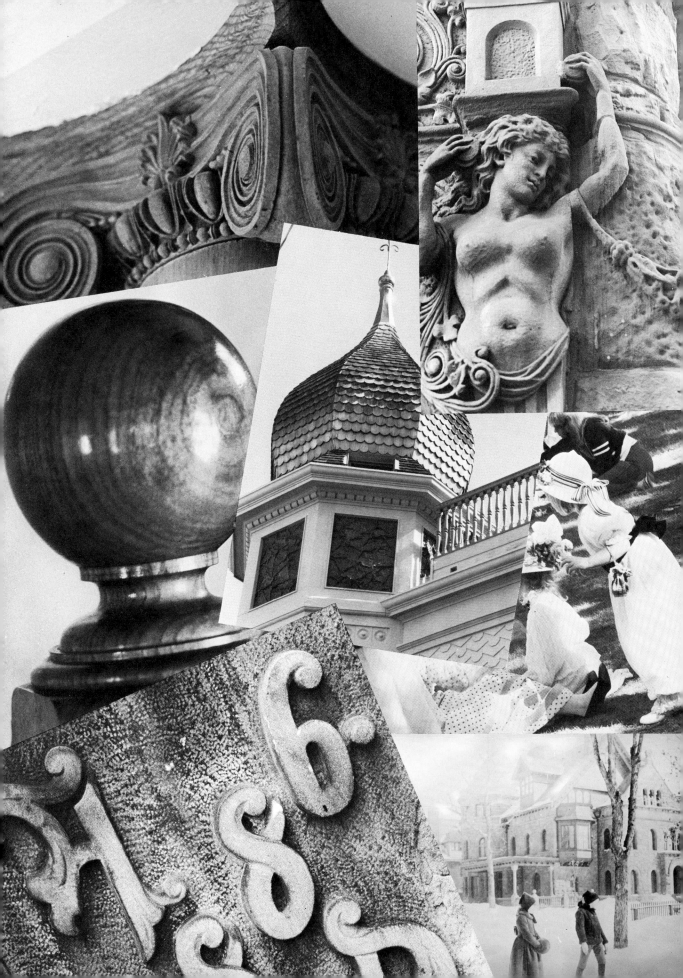

Photo courtesy The Living Historical Museum Macalester College.

PART ONE

I Dream of Home

I dream of quiet days and silent nights, when the
pace of life was slow and people friendly.

I dream of natural things, of solid oak smoothed by
generations of caress and foundations of stone as old as creation.

I dream of other people's dreams, expressed in towers,
turrets, and architectural fancy.

I dream of love, expressed in careful craftsmanship
and the painstaking passion of little things.

I dream of grandfathers and grandmothers, uncles and aunts,
and little children, one of whom could have been me.

I dream of simpler times and simpler places, where
home was where you lived, not what you left.

I dream of the irreplaceable, the incomparable, the stuff
of history that is so easily gone, so difficult to re-create.

I dream of home. I dream of permanence. I dream of a world
now called "old" instead of "good," slipping through my
fingers like half-forgotten memories.

To Find Beauty Again

We are coming home again. We are coming back to the cities, back to our lives that were lived over and over again by people like us.

This old house is me. It is my father's. Or it is one that reminds me of my father, or of his father, or of someone who has lived a life which breathes new life in me.

It is my link to the past, the knot which ties up all the loose ends so efficiently sundered by the long knife of freeways that took my generation or my father's generation on that wild ride to the suburbs.

"New is better," we are told. "Come away from old neighborhoods and old memories. A new house in the country, a new life awaits."

The new split-levels grew like weeds on the scalped suburban earth. New relationships reluctantly developed in the shallow social soil of backyard barbecues. But the frazzled ends of the past lay tangled in dusty trunks still stored in open rafters of the two-car garage.

So we are coming home again. Back to houses built on foundations slowly grown, huge blocks of fieldstone or granite glued with great glops of mortar and the sweat of men and horses. Floors joisted by rough-hewn timbers bigger than the straining muscles of a carpenter's arm. Walls splashed with plaster and horsehair and lath so that nobody could hear the whispers of love at night next door.

And the rooms, the rooms, so big you can swing your arms and jump and bellow with the extravagance of space. Freedom, was that what we were searching for back in our ticky-tack rambler? Here is your freedom, in a room with twelve-foot ceilings and oak wood floors. Room to throw a child overhead in laughter. Studs, cornices, braces, and rafters built to last with nails, screws, and pegs. The freedom of a home, not just a house, sheltered by the knowledge that it has stood for decades and it will stand for more.

It has remained in the good times and the bad. It has seen it all. It has survived. And maybe, with the help of its battered but unbowed history, we shall survive, too.

A home is much more than a house, these old structures teach us. A home is an organism for living, a work of art that expresses our existence. But not a work of art like that of Le Corbusier or Mies van der Rohe, the monumental form-is-function art of hard edges, straight lines, and minimal emotions. Homes are built for people by people, not machines. Homes have soft edges and curved, often crazy, lines.

Homes, the old homes, have character which evolves partly from the builder and mostly from the people who live and shape their lives by the architecture over the years. And because the home has character, it shows its own kind of

We are coming home again, to craftsmanship, to a work of art that expresses our existence.

An old house has character. It shows its own kind of emotion.

emotion, whether it be somber, cheery, mysterious, or restful. With each new family that weds the home, each changes the other to strengthen the sense of character, the sense of history that surrounds the home like shadows.

We are coming home again for more than good, cheap shelter, which many of the deteriorated old structures provide in abundance. We are coming home again for an almost extinct sense of quality. How many times have you heard the phrase "quality of life" scattered like pitchmen's pennies? Probably it was the cliché which took you or your parents from the city in the first place with its promises of sylvan safety, security and freedom from the poor. But modern-building techniques in even the most affluent sub-divisions are more efficient in providing quantity instead of quality. The hollow plasterboard walls ring with an emptiness that can vibrate right into one's own life,

expressing a kind of poverty from which there is no escape.

We go back for craftsmanship, care, individual attention to detail. Does it matter that the floor is full-inch oak or hand-pegged maple? Does it matter that there is a curious carved head peering down from the mantle? Does it matter that the walls are two feet thick, of stone or brick? Does it matter that there are embossed lead downspouts under the decorated eves? Yes, it does matter.

It matters even though the floors may need straightening and the eves may need repair; even though you may have to spend long winter evenings scraping the six coats of paint covering the mantle, as well as the library walls and the kitchen door. It matters that at one time someone had the patience, the skill, and the time to painstakingly perform the art which changes an easily forgotten place of shelter into an irreplaceable sense of place.

We go back to the city to work because an old

The painstaking skill it takes to transform an easily forgotten place of shelter to an irreplaceable sense of place.

home is like an old love: it needs constant attention and tender care. It is expensive to keep up an old house. It takes a certain depth of commitment we aren't usually required to give: Hundreds of dusty hours of cleaning, painting, sanding, and sawing; thousands of dollars spent for the professional help which is beyond our skills. If the assessor or accountant measured the old houses' eroded foundations with his rule of "economic feasibility," very few old structures would be left standing. An old building is restored more with the heart than the head and, usually, only later does the head discover that the heart was right all along.

We go back to friends because old houses express the genius loci, the spirit of the place. And the spirit of the place, as in the past, draws people together. There is no prettier sight for a person struggling to restore an old house than to see someone else down the street doing the same thing. An instant friendship is created with a new language of paint-stripping formulas and carpentry suggestions.

The adversity and adventure of the urban-preservation experience creates a hardy band of like-minded people who celebrate and commiserate together. No matter what a person's income or social status, each is immediately equal in the love of history and the hope of preservation. How many block parties did you have in the suburbs? How many sheetrocking parties, alley clean-ups, midnight pizzas over paint cans?

We come back to the city to find beauty again. This is probably the most ironic and miraculous reason. After all, we went to the suburbs for that reason, didn't we? The flash of a butterfly's wings over a field of green. The splash of a speckled trout in a clear, unpolluted stream. The brilliant blue of a sky uncluttered by TV antennas and sulfur dioxide. That was the original dream the subdividers gave you, wasn't it? Where is it now?

Maybe the city cannot provide you with an un-

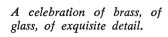

A celebration of brass, of glass, of exquisite detail.

polluted rose garden either. But it can provide a different, probably more lasting, kind of beauty. It is the hidden beauty which history leaves us, the details of an age when even the subdividers' promises were almost true.

The city is still a treasurehouse of detail, those jewels of small perfection which have been overlooked by the Vandal horde of urban renewal, freeways, slumlords, and developers. Now, as the juggernaut of American exploitation is ebbing and as a surprising number of old structures still remain, people scramble back to the city like children delighting over precious shells and seldom-seen creatures in tidal pools. Leaded glass windows with thick beveled panes that sparkle like jewels in the sun.

Parquet floors that almost outdazzle the windows with a kaleidoscope of geometric woods.

A remnant of ancient velvet, heavy with dust and memories.

A door that goes nowhere, yet it is worth the more because it balances a door that opens to the kitchen in a symmetrical dining room.

The celebration of brass: doorknobs, window

The wood—sawed, planed, carved, mortised, pegged. It makes you gasp, and something called history suddenly has meaning.

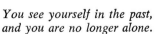

You see yourself in the past, and you are no longer alone.

locks, name plates, light switches, kitchen lamps, toilet pulls, coat hooks.

And the wood, the wood. White oak. Maple. Mahogany, as many kinds as the world holds. Pine. Beech. Birch. Cherry. Sawed. Planed. Sanded. Carved. Mortised. Pegged.

Oiled and waxed. Rubbed and stroked by mothers and fathers and grand uncles and aunts until you touch it and it makes you gasp, and something called history suddenly has meaning.

Who are we? What do we want to become? How can we know if we don't know where we have been. How can we know it is us?

Moving back to the city is a journey which cannot be measured in miles. Going back to the city, going back to an old house which has sheltered generations, can become a journey back to one's own roots. A sense of history is more than old photographs of people long dead. A sense of history is like a mirror which one holds up to oneself.

You look past the old photograph or old walls of a house and you see yourself in the context of the past.

You are no longer alone.

You are part of a heritage which had purpose and a meaning then. It has even more meaning, more value, now, because you are a part of it.

Roots. They provide stability for the plant and help it to grow. They hold protectively and give freedom at the same time. History gives us roots. By making history and its artifacts part of our lives, we in turn become a significant part of history. And by understanding a little better our place in history, we may find it easier to face the future.

Is this too much to ask of an old house? Of course it is. We can only enjoy an old house for what it is and what we make of it, as a good investment, a good place in which to live.

But as we become comfortable with the history of the place, the spirit of the place, we may also be able to ask a little more of ourselves.

Maybe, as we renew the dusty, funky old house, we may also be engaged in the process of renewing ourselves.

Maybe, as we renew the dusty, funky old house, we may also renew ourselves.

PART TWO

Where It's Happening

Recent statistics * show that 75 per cent of all large American cities are experiencing the restoration of old buildings, as well as one half of all smaller cities. Statistics show that of the 23 million housing units in America, five million are deteriorated. Statistics show that the young, the white, the middle-class, and upper-income people have renovated over 58,000 of those old houses between 1968 and 1974.

But the cold light of statistics can't illuminate the real drama now being enacted in almost every town and hamlet, as well as major city, in America. The statistics are like wind chimes on your back porch which say the air is moving but do not tell whether the breeze is momentary or the fore-whisper of a hurricane.

As a lover of old buildings and a restorer of them, as an admirer of old neighborhoods and an avid preserver of them, I too had felt the stirring of a new consciousness and a new power in America. Conversations with other old-house conservationists, news items in the morning paper, and the latest statistics only whetted my appetite to know, to see, to experience the reality of the neighborhood preservation movement in America. Was the restoring of old buildings just a passing fad of a few élitist dilettantes? Did the "gentrification" of former slums mean another displacement of the poor residents on their eternal journey

* Urban Land Institute study, 1977.

to nowhere? And if there was a back-to-the-city movement, why did the statistics still show urban population to be declining? Who is coming back to the city, and who is leaving?

To try to answer these questions, I decided to ask the people who could most reasonably answer them—the men and women who are on the front lines of urban revitalization, personally restoring and rehabilitating old houses and commercial buildings from Portland, Oregon, to Portland, Maine; from St. Paul to San Antonio. I also wanted to ask the people who were already living there, in those neighborhoods statisticians and politicians call slums.

The result was a ten-thousand-mile visit to over two dozen cities and towns in the United States, and conversations with hundreds of people involved in neighborhood preservation. The reception amid plaster dust and wood shavings, half-restored townhouses and magnificently completed homes, was gracious. The answers and impressions were genuine and exciting. By freezing the current national preservation experience in the amber of immediacy, these impressions may help us examine the process and potential of this extraordinary phenomenon a little more closely.

The first and most overwhelming impression of the homes and neighborhoods being fixed up in America is one of magnitude. The so-called urban-preservation movement seems to be the most dynamic grass-roots, populist expression by the American people since the great westward agrarian movement of the late 1800s. It is not only a movement by suburbanites back to the city, although the returning of suburban people is significant. It is also a "stay in the city" movement, with urban-oriented people or their sons and daughters opting to stay in neighborhoods others have abandoned, rehabilitating structures others have neglected.

Another refreshing impression is its truly grass-roots character. Often a house or neighborhood is restored in spite of the local-, state-, and federal-government agencies which are supposedly empowered to "renew" communities. Lonely individuals, faced with indifference if not the outright antagonism of almost every form of the American power structure, are fighting and winning the battle of owning a neglected home and improving a "red lined" neighborhood. Almost every preservationist in every city has his or her favorite horror story of governmental "urban renewal" projects which laid waste to acres of beautiful old buildings, of the city councils or chambers of commerce which preferred freeways or industrial parks to neighborhoods, of the bureaucratic red tape which works to strangle any attempt at restoring or re-using an old building.

Yet surprisingly, the inmates are beginning to take over the asylum. The governed are beginning to relearn the fact that American democracy empowers a government by the people and for the people. The often almost deserted inner city is developing a constituency again of active, intelligent, and vocal residents. As a lady in Savannah said, "The government experts have to be educated by the uneducated."

The residents, the rehabbers, the schoolteachers and carpenters and nurses and sometimes unemployed are deciding that there is indeed value in old buildings and run-down neighborhoods. Then they are going through the long and painful process of educating the politicians and pundits who control the destiny of a community: the city council, city planning, and urban development departments, bankers, insurance executives, federal-funding officials, and even the local police department.

The process of restoring a neighborhood is a process of communication, of education. Not only do new ways to strip old wallpaper need to be learned, but new values and new attitudes about living need to be embraced. People are coming back to the city as one who returns to face the remnants of a drunken party of the night before. It seems as if all America, after the disastrous economic depression of the 1930s and the victorious war of the 1940s, had decided to go on a decade-long binge of consuming our natural and built resources. There was a gargantuan gorging of new suburban subdivisions, new automobiles and the four-lane freeways to run them on, and a new consumer mentality to "think young." Old houses and neighborhoods became so much soiled Kleenex, ready to be plowed under by the federally primed juggernaut of Urban Renewal.

But the party is over now. Not only the cities but the surrogate suburbs are stumbling around with a gigantic hangover of vanquished hopes in the debris of poverty, crime, and a smog-enshrouded future. The lessons are having to be learned over again that there is no free lunch or free party. Money alone cannot buy decent housing or the fragile complexity of a successful community. It takes people. It takes their personal commitment, their active involvement in the community process, and the willingness of the local power structure to work with them.

The following are just a few examples of cities where the exquisite contradictions of the urban revitalization movement are taking place. Maybe as we learned after the throw-away 1940s and 50s and 60s that there is no free lunch, we are now learning that there are no easy answers. Each successful restoration or rehabilitation project in each community seems to be unique. We discover that often the "urban pioneers" are not returning to the city but have never left the city. We discover that even the term "preservation" is giving way to the more populist term of "conservation" in describing what is happening to the old communities. And our image of the upper-income, white, urban pioneer bringing light and beauty back to deteriorated neighborhoods and his neighbors is tempered by the equally valid image of the poor, the Black, the Puerto Rican street gang also professionally and sensitively restoring the old buildings and the urban quality of life.

Yet these contradictions only heighten the positive and healthy process that is building in each of these cities, unique preservation experiences which act like the binding of strong weft with the ever-creating warp of our American urban tapestry.

We have learned there are limits to our American dream. We are rediscovering the treasures still available in our cities and towns, not just the old buildings, but the exciting mixture that happens when architecture and people get together, work together, in all the glorious diversity of age, income, color, and interests. The mixture, the rubbing together of shoulders and ideas and attitudes, is what makes these towns and cities so exciting, so worthwhile to remain in and to return to.

A Celebration of Victorians:
San Francisco

They call it Bagdad by the Bay, and one can sense a legendary, unreal quality about San Francisco. As the afternoon sun strikes the riot of colors on the freshly painted wooden Victorian homes that march up the hills from the sea, the cares of the present seem suspended by the magic of a re-created past. In spite of a spectacular modern commercial downtown with its Gateway Center and the Transamerica Pyramid and Hyatt Regency Hotel, this golden city is still nineteenth-century at its very best.

There are over two thousand historically significant Victorian-style buildings still standing on these hills bordered by the Pacific Ocean and San Francisco Bay, over thirteen thousand Victorians still of fine architectural quality, and thousands more hidden under layers of 1930s and 1950s remodelings. Today, entire blocks, entire

The hillsides are alive with color. The eclectic old Victorian architecture glows with yellows and greens and browns, sometimes seven hues at once.

A forest of scaffolding rises along San Francisco streets. Old houses are being repainted, reroofed, restored, transforming entire neighborhoods from almost deserted slums into bustling, beautiful communities.

neighborhoods, are undergoing a massive, individually financed restoration effort, building by building. There is a preservation, a return-to-the-city movement here that one can almost feel. It is hard to ignore as scaffolding rises against the old houses like a new kind of free-form, kinetic sculpture.

This exuberance seems to be more western, more eclectic than in many parts of the country, possibly because here the struggle to survive, let alone preserve, has been so great. The 1906 earthquake destroyed many structures, and the subsequent fire destroyed thousands more. Yet even this greatest American earthquake did not do as great damage to San Francisco's architectural heritage as have more recent political decisions in the name of "urban renewal." In the 1960s, an entire community of Victorian homes was de-

stroyed, twenty-eight square blocks of five thousand of the best Victorians in San Francisco's Western Addition. These irreplaceable redwood houses were replaced with typical modern housing, three-story stucco apartments which a perceptive British architect calls "Los Angeles Dingbat."

We were losing the city we loved, so we decided to fight.

As has happened all over America, it often takes a spectacularly gross, utterly destructive blow to a community's physical and social character before the public will react. The destruction of the Western Addition suddenly made the fabric of the city, its old homes, visible again. For years

San Francisco preservationists were losing old architecture through neglect and demolition. Their decision to fight back has created a systematic campaign for sensitizing people to the beauty of old houses and old neighborhoods.

borhoods through recognition of the historic and architectural value of their houses. It also helped residents see that their old houses had more value in their original state than with what Judith has termed "misguided improvements." Some of the finest old houses were covered with stucco, aluminum, or phony asbestos brick siding while elaborate hand-carved window bays and front porches were removed to give the house a "modern" look. Over six thousand of the Victorians were hidden by the clutzy results of a 1950s siding-salesman's dream.

You can't believe the neighborhoods, how they've transformed themselves.

The education of the city's residents to their architectural heritage has worked miracles. The last Victorian house was torn down in 1974, thanks to an outraged citizenry. The era of "urban renewal" is over in San Francisco, and now a slow and delicate process of urban restoration is underway.

they had been taken for granted, lived in and tolerated, but not cherished. But the death of a community and the resultant despair of its residents and a city of old-house lovers caused a transformation of public consciousness.

One of the key efforts at identifying the architectural treasure which the city still contained was accomplished by Judith Waldhorn, an urbanologist and admirer of Victorian architecture. Thanks to a $10,000 grant from the National Endowment for the Arts, she was able to survey 13,487 Victorian houses still standing on the hills of the city. From that survey, she compiled a series of publications and walking tours about the San Francisco Victorians.

Because of efforts such as hers and the nonprofit Foundation for San Francisco's Architectural Heritage, the historic housing of the city and its surrounding neighborhoods were more fully identified. Residents were able to develop a stronger sense of place and pride in their neigh-

Judith Waldhorn knows many of the 13,487 San Francisco Victorian houses by name. Thanks to the efforts of her and her friends, most of the architecturally important houses have been identified, even behind the camouflage of "misguided improvements."

One of the new types of restoration specialist helping neighborhoods regain their Victorian-style streetscapes is Hal Majors, head of a firm called the Preservation Group. They purchase badly deteriorated houses, often left vacant for years and stripped of most architectural details, and then restore or reconstruct the structures for residential or commercial use.

Restoration developers such as the Preservation Group take on projects no typical developer would think of touching, because old house restoration can become some of the world's most complicated construction projects. As in Major's experience, an old house may first have to be moved from its original site where it may have stood vacant for twenty years, and then its interior studs may have to be replaced because of rot, while most of its intricate architectural details may have to be replaced because of vandalism.

A construction cost estimate is impossible, so the contractor must reassess every step of the job, plan creative solutions to impossible problems, and hope that someone will pay the price which the final mountain of unforeseen costs will total.

And to increase the complexity of the operation, a building may have to be beautifully painted even before it is moved, and before real construction begins, just to prove to the potential bank financer that the building is worth restoring in the first place. For a building that has already withstood earthquakes, fires and years of neglect, it usually is all worth it.

The house wasn't pretty and we wanted to make it pretty.

Steve and Terry Silverman are restoring their second Victorian home on the hills above the Mission District. They exemplify a special trait which most old-house lovers seem to have; a secure enough image of themselves so they can even be attracted to an "ugly duckling" of a house, knowing that underneath all the grime and misguided improvements is a thing of beauty.

Why do so many people leave the deteriorating city in the first place? Could it be that they did not want to be identified with the old, the growing ugliness of deterioration? Today the preserva-

Hal Majors and his Preservation Group are among the few specialists who are restoring old houses and then reselling or leasing them for commercial and residential use. The structures behind him are part of a recycled complex called The Phelps Place Historic Plaza.

Because of the pressure of new development, many historic houses have to be either demolished or moved. The ability to cut through the red tape needed to move a house, and then to satisfy all the building codes during reconstruction, has become a high art among preservationists.

tionist looks past the ugliness and is enchanted by the creative, constructive process which becomes beauty.

The Silvermans would never consider living outside the city. They like the feeling of being in the middle of things, the many choices of cultural activities, the many friends who live close-by. They didn't even know they were part of a "movement" to restore inner-city neighborhoods. When they bought their first Victorian after Steve graduated from college, they were just looking for a house they could afford. They only discovered later that the sense of warmth, the sense of humanity which attracted them to the first little house was an expression of its history. And then they began to see the house not simply as an accumulation of boards and braces and beams. It became a work of ancient art, a sculpture which brings out the latent creativity in the owner.

With the second house, after their two young children made the first little Carpenter Gothic too small, they began to realize the impact old houses have on people's lives. Terry tells of the joy of walking into the still grimy, still pioneer neighborhoods on the San Francisco hills, where you open a front door and it's like walking into sunshine. The richness of Victorian detail and embellishments hidden in these unprepossessing houses staggers one who has become sensitive to their charm.

To the Silvermans, their home has become an expression of themselves. They respond to the warmth and human scale of the old house, seek-

The Silvermans are happily restoring their second Victorian Queen-Anne style row house. They consider themselves "city people" and wouldn't think of living anywhere but on the hills of San Francisco. (Photo courtesy Judith Waldhorn.)

ing a passion in its architecture which is lacking in the glass and sterile austerity of modern buildings. Contemporary architects seem to be still wedded to the Bauhaus design concept of the 1920s with its cool lines, right angles, and primary colors. The less-is-more philosophy of Walter Gropius and Marcel Breuer and Mies van der Rohe somehow lost its humanity while searching for the perfect uncluttered line. Now the post-Watergate, post-Suburban Split-level generation of Americans look for a better way of living back where it all started, in the historic inner cities.

The best housing that we will ever hope to have in our cities is nineteenth-century housing.

Gary Kray says that San Francisco is one of the most desirable cities in the world in which to live, and it has the finest housing ever created. He speaks with some authority because he is founding partner of San Francisco Victoriana, possibly the nation's first total-service manufacturer and contractor for authentic Victorian building restoration and embellishment.

What began a few years ago as an effort to reproduce a few Victorian architectural details for people interested in replacing a lost or damaged finial, molding, or oak-detailed front door has now become a full-scale operation that can authentically restore or reconstruct a Victorian front porch or an entire authentic-down-to-the-last-baluster Victorian home. And they do it with all natural materials, using original nineteenth-century lathes and designs.

Gary feels that they are re-establishing pride in old neighborhoods that had none. Even the Haight-Ashbury area of the city, which was once the symbol of the birth and then the death of the flower-child hopes of the 1960s, is now boasting restored streets of Victorian houses and a new kind of quality of life. He says that his firm is involved in much the same kind of reconstruction of historic San Francisco as was the reconstruction of the bombed-out European cities after the Second World War. They, and it seems as if almost all of San Francisco, are now putting the city and its architectural heritage back together

Gary Kray feels that he and his associates are re-creating San Francisco's golden age, bringing Victorian architecture to life in a modern context. He now waits for the ultimate Victorian buff to ask him to build an authentic Queen Anne from foundation up.

again. Reason enough for the houses on the hills to celebrate.

People are gaining a greater sense of personal freedom as they explore the potential of a house.

Although many people across the nation are beginning to create a more personal and contemporary interior environment inside historic old houses, San Francisco seems to especially symbolize changing attitudes about the ethics and values of historic preservation. Of course, historic

Victorian kitchens need not be dark and dreary. Bernadine, Harry, and son, Jimmy Barry, enjoy their crystal kitchen windows created by artist Bruce Sherman. (Photo courtesy Judith Waldhorn.)

preservation first began on the East Coast where much of the concern and interest in saving old houses was with the intention of returning them, inside and out, to their original period in history. For example, in the Park Slope neighborhood of Brooklyn, the brownstones have been beautifully and very intricately restored. Much of the furniture is period furniture and even the knickknacks and accessories are all exquisite period pieces. The homes are enjoyed as homes, but also there is a museum quality about them.

However, in San Francisco, and increasingly in other parts of the nation, old-house preservation is taking on a more personal celebration quality. There is a certain spontaneity and creativity in the preservation process where the intent is not to carefully preserve the structure and its contents exactly. There is a respect for the architectural integrity of the structure, especially the exterior, and respect for the historical quality in the interior to a degree, but there is more eclecticism and a new free-form use of interior space which expresses the individual's interests and lifestyle.

The houses are viewed as more utilitarian, causing the efforts of historic preservation to become more utilitarian. And slowly but surely, the philosophy of urban historic restoration or preservation becomes one of urban conservation—using houses for what houses are traditionally used for, respecting the architectural integrity and their unique design, but still making them one's own. This is especially dramatized in the use of coloration on the San Francisco Victorians, where the many colorful combinations of paint make each house a very personal expression of the owner. Surprisingly, this does not detract from the streetscape or detract from the historical quality of the house. Instead it popularizes and humanizes the essential character of the home.

We still need the historically authentic house museums as we need the people who enjoy living in a home that is historically accurate in the interior as well as the exterior. But, fortunately, today we are in an age when we can realistically think of saving not just one historic building but cities full of them. And in order to accomplish this, cities of people must get involved, from architectural historians to people who simply want an old house they can call their own. Then, in our own individualistic American fashion, we will prove that whatever once was beautiful, or whatever once was enjoyable, there's no reason why it can't be enjoyable and beautiful again.

Building the Future from the Past: St. Paul

Running broad and beautifully through the middle of the Historic Hill District of St. Paul, Minnesota, elm-lined Summit Avenue proves that one of the finest historic residential streets in the nation can survive. It begins at the Cathedral of St. Paul which overlooks the center city and ends five miles later at the edge of the Mississippi River, a showplace of architectural extravagance, a history of the affluence of the city from the Federal and Greek Revival styles of the 1840s to the Jacobean and Provincial adaptions of the 1930s.

Spreading out from this towered and turreted street of mansions and churches is a watershed of progressively smaller homes built by the assistants, shopkeepers, and servants of the great St. Paul families. Even these homes, although not created by architects of the stature of a Cass Gilbert, still express the individuality and spontaneity of pine and brick designs taken from Victorian and Carpenter Gothic-style pattern books.

But in the late 1960s, the exuberance of Summit Avenue was seedy and subdued. Many grand homes then contained rabbit warrens of efficiency apartments, some homes were abandoned, others mysteriously burned to leave a gaping hole in this priceless historic streetscape. And just a few blocks to the north, the desolation was even greater, causing the city fathers to begin a classic urban renewal effort of demolishing the still sturdy but neglected homes. After an expenditure of $44 million on "renewal," a 1973 study titled *Document of a Dilemma* reported that the effort had "destroyed more housing than it created, displaced more families than it has sheltered, and has generally left vacant structures or empty spaces where residential neighborhoods once existed. The impact of this wholesale elimination of buildings and persons brings the picture of a bombed-out city to mind—the disorientation must be similar, the atmosphere of a community in trauma nearly identical."

We thought we were buying a home, but discovered that the neighborhood came with the deal.

Yet while this seemingly irreversible process of deterioration and destruction was happening, a few young couples began to purchase homes on or near the still relatively genteel Summit Avenue. The charm of the architecture and the magnificence of the interior spaces of their newly discovered homes blinded them to the sense of discouragement and destruction which hung in the neighborhood air like smoke from another charred home.

James and Margaret Lynden are two of these early new and unexpected residents who moved

Summit Avenue was called "the street of empire builders." Along its five miles of broad avenue and parklike lawns, the march of majestic architecture documents the growth of the city and the Western nation from 1840 to the 1900s.

back to the city from the affluent suburb of Edina, much to the amazement of their friends as well as the older Historic Hill residents who were still grimly holding on to their homes.

The Lyndens didn't think of themselves as particularly brave or visionary at the time. The somewhat shabby three-story Victorian frame house with its matching carriage house and big yard was very attractively priced. And as often happens to people who get too close to an old house, they simply fell in love with the place, with its past, its promise, and the potential for gracious living it held.

It was only later, after the first glow of owning a home subsided and they saw two or three houses

What was an old carriage house has become a spectacular apartment. Jim, Margaret, and son, John Lynden, hold the landscaping design which will link their Historic Hill home with its new income property.

fall around them daily, due to the wrecking ball or vandalism, that the new arrivals began to organize. Joining forces with the older residents, they formed neighborhood associations: the Summit Hill Association in 1967, the Lexington/Hamline Community Council in 1968, the Ramsey Hill Association in 1972, and the Portland Avenue Association in 1974. Jim Lynden and his neighbors helped write and have enacted state legislation in 1973 which created the entire six-square-mile area as the Historic Hill District. Margaret and her friends organized house tours to show both residents and outsiders that the community still had beauty and value. Although they expected a few hundred visitors, thousands came. And this personal approach, the pragmatic proving to the uneducated just what value old houses could provide, became the key effort in the reawakening of the vast suburban mentality to the potential of a new kind of urban ethic.

This new coalition of recent and old residents also formed a nonprofit corporation called Old Town Restorations, Inc., which was dedicated to the preservation and improvement of the community. This led to the creation of the Historic Hill District Planning Program, a community-based, interdisciplinary planning and implementation program which helped identify the architectural and historical qualities of the community and formed a series of programs to improve the quality of life of the area.

You have to have a sense of where you are. You have to have a desire to be part of the community.

Irene and John Tittle are examples of young couples who have come later. The easiest homes to sell were the large, still fairly well-maintained mansions along the relatively safe avenue. But many of the streets to the north were still battle-grounds of poverty and despair. The smaller Carpenter Gothic and Prairie Farm House-style homes had been abandoned, butchered.

An Historic Hill Planning Program study in the spring of 1976 identified 130 vacant and boarded structures in the northern half of the Historic Hill. By September of 1977, only one

John and Irene Tittle (with the newest member of the family) are restoring a home in one of the most badly deteriorated parts of the Hill. They like their neighborhood with its diversity, they say, and wouldn't live anywhere else.

was left that was not being restored. Some had been vacant for years. Even though they were priced at only a few thousand dollars for a twelve- or twenty-room house, prior to the restoration efforts of 1976 no one would buy them.

Today, they are still the same homes on the same streets. Yet they are now selling for three to ten times their earlier market value. The only real thing that has changed is the attitude of the people who live there. They see themselves as part of a community that has value, owning homes that have value, living on a street that contains people who they know and can rely on. A sense of community has evolved from a sense of despair. People now can see a future for themselves and their children in a community which only a couple of years earlier had no future.

Today, John and Irene are not only personally restoring their own home. They have purchased a couple of other houses in the neighborhood which everyone else had given up on. They have made a complete, personal commitment to their neighborhood by rehabilitating its real estate. John was asked, What is real estate? And his answer was: Real estate is those pieces of property which lie within a certain geographical area which has certain physical, social, and economic characteristics. You can't divide the one from the other. And that is what neighborhoods are all about, why people form neighborhood associations. People feel they are a neighborhood of

unique people and structures, as opposed to being a subdivision or a suburb. Their uniqueness gives themselves and their structures value that goes far beyond what speculators and assessors traditionally consider "real estate."

We can handle the petty thievery and harassment. But it's when you come up against

John Tittle does most of the work on his house himself. He is proud that he has learned to be a good carpenter, proud of his own sweat that has gone into his home.

a city council or school board which does not understand or participate in the neighborhood, yet has a tremendous amount of power over it, that is where the problems are.

The universal difference in neighborhoods which are in the process of restoration is the involvement, the enthusiasm of the residents. Peter Quinn lives down the street from John Tittle. He also is restoring his home. He also has purchased a couple of badly deteriorated houses.

Like most people restoring old houses in the area, he has little money but great energy and imagination. He does most of the work himself, employing local young people to help him with the difficult jobs of knocking down plaster and hauling debris. All he asks is that people care about the old houses and appreciate the new vitality that is growing in the neighborhood.

It is especially frustrating when some people see the improvements in the area, but don't believe what they see. They are untouched by the changes which will be of benefit to themselves and to the city. They refuse to get involved.

One lady has lived in the neighborhood for seventeen years. Restoration is going all around her, yet she still won't fix her roof after seventeen years. She still won't believe that things are improving. She put up a big chain link ghetto fence around her house that is eight feet high. She still expects the neighborhood to go to hell. She buys no possessions because she thinks someone is going to steal them. She has an alarm system in the house and multiple locks on her doors. Peter and John hope that some day she will come out of the house and talk with them. Maybe then, they think, she will lose her fear and believe that things are getting better.

It's everybody's childhood dream to live in a mansion on Summit Avenue. This has come the closest to being that of anything I have had the opportunity to own.

Roger Opp lives just around the corner from Summit Avenue in one of four three-story town-

Peter Quinn says that fixing up your own house is only part of the job. Helping to fix up the neighborhood around it, getting to know the people and solving the problems, that's the biggest job of all.

houses that used to house twelve low-rent apartments. Author F. Scott Fitzgerald lived just down the street and he too used to dream of enjoying the special magic that seems to come from owning these middle-class castles of brick and stone.

Roger, single, a business analyst born in a rural Minnesota town, fell in love with the gigantic building, enchanted at just the thought of owning a piece of a large building like that. He lived in its vacant three stories and basement for a year, camping out, waiting for the building to tell him what to do with it, waiting to gather the courage to make the tremendous financial commitment he knew it would take to turn the empty nearly one-hundred-year-old spaces into a home for him.

The marvelous thing about an old building is its space. A badly deteriorated interior can be a blessing in disguise, allowing one to use the space in new and exciting ways, as shown here in Roger Opp's townhouse.

Finally, he gathered the courage and a large loan from a friendly home-town banker. With the encouragement and advise of Tim Geisler, a local young architect, Roger gutted the basement and first floor while he continued to live in the upper half of the building. He laughs with a good deal of amazement as he realizes that he is spending more in the rehabilitation of his building that his father may have spent in his entire life. A naturally quiet and conservative person, he realizes that his emotions ran away with his better sense. But, he reflects, he is glad it happened that way, glad that his home, which is now blossoming into a spectacularly beautiful duplex, made him do it.

Roger Opp camped out in his vacant building for a year, waiting for it to tell him what to do. He's glad he waited now, happy to own a home that is uniquely his.

"Government money is a very uneven match for the spirit of a city's people."

The $44 million spent in the early St. Paul urban renewal effort is only a small part of the billions spent by the federal government in other cities. But the general lack of success in these bureaucratic efforts is universal. Many city offi-

cials still can't understand why massive injections of money can't stabilize a community.

If you were to ask Louie Sudheimer why, he may reply that residents of a community usually want to do things themselves, in their own way. They want to be part of the decision-making process, part of the re-creation of a community. Louie and his wife, Pam, were part of the creation of Old Town Restorations, Inc., and the His-

This was a single-story boiler room for a Historic Hill apartment building. It is now a two-story home with an outsize chimney that adds to its charm.

toric Hill program. He was also one of the people who developed the first Old Town rehabilitation project of saving the apartment house birthplace of F. Scott Fitzgerald. He was also involved in saving another apartment building which was burned, vandalized, and slated for demolition. Dubbed "The Phoenix," it recently won an award for being the best rehabilitated housing for the money spent.

Like many of his neighbors, his restoration efforts have become a way of life. He quit his well-paying job to continue to restore other buildings. Other Hill residents have left banking positions to become carpenters, government jobs to become contractors. The pioneering spirit opens up new options for people, new possibilities for the use of one's time and talent.

Today, the new pioneers of St. Paul gather in

The restoration, by Old Town Restorations, Inc., of the apartment building where F. Scott Fitzgerald was born began what has become the most active restoration of old multiple dwellings for condominiums in the nation.

Pam and Louie Sudheimer progressed from restoring their own home to restoring other deteriorated buildings in the area. Here they prepare for an open house in their St. Albans Court Condominiums.

the backyards and front porches of homes that once housed earlier pioneers. They compare paint-stripping formulas and neighborhood news. Although more houses are being repaired, more streets made safe to stroll on at night, the winning of the Hill is still going on. There always seems to be another old house to save from demolition on the next street down, another politician to convince that St. Paul is really a nice place to live.

"But things must be getting better," muses one paint-spattered woman as she raises her glass. "A state congressman just moved on my block."

There comes a time when you've just got to do something a little crazy, like fixing up an abandoned house.

The Historic Hill District is not the only place where heroic efforts of neighborhood revitalization are occurring, just as the Lyndens and the Tittles are not the only people involved. Just below the Hill, next to the Mississippi River and in the shadow of the high-rise bank buildings downtown, is a tiny park surrounded by old frame homes from the 1880s and earlier in various stages of repair.

This is Irvine Park, the oldest residential section surviving in St. Paul. Earlier slated for

Everybody gets involved when an old house needs fixing. The Marhoun family of Irvine Park feel that moving back to the city made them a better family as well as better carpenters.

Although many interiors of restored St. Paul homes are traditional, this Dayton Avenue residence is an example of the dramatic transformation an old building can offer.

A few years ago, many structures were either burned, boarded, abandoned, or were so deteriorated that they were unsafe and unhealthful. Today, many of the same buildings now welcome Historic Hill residents to a better way of life.

demolition, the city was finally encouraged to sell the badly deteriorated and often abandoned buildings for $1 each to people who would renovate them.

George Marhoun, his wife, Peggy, and sons, Mark and Rick, were the first Irvine Park pioneers to move into their new home. As with most of the new residents, they are working on the house as they live in it. For two years, "home" has been open rafters and sawdust, the smell of paint and turpentine.

Yet for the Marhouns, Irvine Park has been the greatest experience in their lives. Their former existence in a safe, middle-class suburb seems so far away now. The new/old house has focused their family life; the promise of the time when it finally will be completely painted, nailed, and plumbed has focused their future.

They and their neighbors are some of the lucky ones who had the courage and imagination to be part of the rebirth of a city. Now visitors drive into town on a Sunday afternoon, marveling at the transformations in Irvine Park and on the Hill and West Seventh Street and dozens more of other-century pockets of old homes being restored. They see the pioneers like the Marhouns standing on their front porches and wonder, "Why didn't I have the sense to buy an old house when they were cheap and I had the chance? Why couldn't I have the satisfaction of watching the Johnny-come-latelies driving by?"

A Queen Anne "witch's hat" reconstructed and about to crown a beautifully restored home in St. Paul's Irvine Park.

A Historic City Hidden Among High-rises: Chicago

Chicago, Carl Sandburg's "city of broad shoulders, hog butcher to the world," has shown many faces to the stranger. It is a city of seedy slums and dreary high-rise ghettos of the poor if one drives through parts of south Chicago or the near northwest. It is a city of the Magnificent Mile and spectacular new architecture in the central city. Linked to the Gold Coast to the north, it is one of the healthiest downtowns in the United States. Chicago has pioneered the new, the modern, the trend-setting architectural styles since Louis Sullivan was teaching his student Frank Lloyd Wright. And this boisterous city has thought little of knocking down the old to make way for the newer, the taller, the more spectacular.

But people often overlook the continuity of impact which historic preservation has made and is making to strengthen Chicago's economic vigor. People are remaining in the city, and moving back to it, thanks in part to historic urban neighborhoods which often are overlooked in the high-rise, high-income splendor of Chicago's Gold Coast.

One of the most dramatic and long-lived stories of successful neighborhood preservation has occurred in a seven-neighborhood area just north of Chicago's Loop, called the Lincoln Park Conservation Area. Next to a large lakefront park on the east, and some still badly deteriorated communities to the west, it has survived the exodus of the middle class from the city in the 1950s, the urban renewal destruction of the 1960s, and now the massive new-development activity of the 1970s. This small band of Lincoln Park neighborhoods not only symbolizes the success of longevity of nineteenth-century homes, they are also the living memorial to the true, historic identity of the city of Chicago.

Before Chicago became the city of innovative high-rise architecture and big ideas, it was known as the City in a Garden. The official city seal still proclaims "Urbs in Harto." Few of the town's inhabitants in the 1830s, or the visitor today, could identify the old city in its modern guise of slums, grime, and traffic chaos. Few could, that is, if they do not find their way to the Near North Side, the other-century world of the Lincoln Park communities.

This cast-iron garden gate is the symbol of the Lincoln Park community, the one area that still represents historic Chicago when it was known as "the city in a garden."

We were originally a community of truck gardens, and we don't forget it.

The area was first settled in the 1850s by German truck gardeners. The small wooden farmhouses were almost all destroyed in the great Chicago fire of 1871. Almost immediately after the fire, the residents built a more urban environment for themselves, from wooden "relief shanties" and small brick cottages in the south and west, to more imposing townhouses and stone mansions to the north.

But what this community did not forget was its city-in-a-garden heritage. Most of the newly built 1870s and 1880s Victorian-style homes kept a little garden in their backyards and about fifteen feet of grass and shrubs in their front yards. Much of the area is a community designed for neighborliness, for children to play in cozy backyards. And even in the bad years, when the area stopped growing in the early 1900s and began to deteriorate as a new wave of immigrants moved in, many of the original German, Polish, and Scandinavian families held on to their homes and community.

Some of the small apartments and townhouses were converted into rooming houses. Light manufacturing downgraded the character of some of the streets which formerly housed small shops. An elevated railroad dissected part of the community. By the Second World War, the old middle-class residents were barely holding their own against the growing force of deterioration and increasing absentee-landlord neglect. As Chicago was growing bigger, the old Near North Side neighborhoods were growing shabbier and weaker in power.

Yet at this critical time, two events combined to help revitalize the community. Thanks to the residents' truck-gardening heritage and their still-existing backyard gardens, the wartime concept of Victory gardens began to unite the neighborhoods in a common cause. At the same time, newcomers discovered these attractive neighborhoods, and Chicago's original "back to the city" movement began. The urban pioneers of the 1940s, as is frequently the case today, were the artists, the young professionals. Radio personalities from the old radio shows became Lincoln Park residents, as did Johnny Weismuller who was "Tarzan" of the movies, and historian Paul Angle.

With the war over, the old and new residents turned their attention from organizing Victory garden activities to organizing concern for the preservation and improvement of their community. The Lincoln Park Community Association was born, and for over thirty years one of the nation's oldest active neighborhood-improvement associations has worked to make the Near North section of Chicago one of the most active and effective Historic Districts in the nation.

You're an Old Towner if you can hear the bells of St. Michael's.

Maurice Forkert lives in the Old Town Triangle neighborhood of the larger Lincoln Park community. He has been active in the umbrella Lincoln Park organization since the Victory garden days. He remembers the victory celebrations after the war and the general community consensus that if they could work together during the war to help win a victory over the Axis, they could continue to work together in times of peace to win the battle over neighborhood deterioration.

Maurice Forkert stands before his 1872 residence. A blend of Swiss and Victorian styling, its wide overhanging veranda supported by elaborately carved brackets expresses both the quality and the eclecticism of many Lincoln Park homes.

So the neighborhoods banded together to fight the city's Department of Urban Renewal in order to keep the bulldozers out of their community. Then they fought for Historic Designation of their neighborhoods, public funds for community improvements, and private investors to purchase and rehabilitate the flophouses and abandoned buildings.

The results achieved by Forkert and his neighbors, although the battle is continuing, have been impressive. In just his Old Town Triangle neighborhood of 625 homes, private investment and improvement of the old houses, which were calculated by actual building permits during the last fifteen years, amounts to over $200 million. This is an expression of historic preservation by private individuals using private money which even the accountants in City Hall can understand.

Forkert feels that part of the success in his neighborhood is due to the strong identity residents have with their community. The streets of Queen Anne-style row houses and Eastlake-style frame homes surround a major landmark and reminder of the neighborhood's past. St. Michael's Church was built by the German-Catholic residents in 1869. The Chicago fire in 1871 destroyed it, but before the rubble had barely cooled, the parish was already at work restoring the gutted building to its original form. Like the community around it, the church has been refurbished and redecorated repeatedly over the years, but its bells pealing from its tower constantly remind people of their historic past and their lively present. According to local lore, anyone who can hear the bells of St. Michael's is an "Old Towner." Today's residents, no matter what their age, religion, race, or income, take personal pride in St. Michael's and the heritage it proclaims.

Many of the streets in the Old Town Triangle are quiet, tree shaded, ending in cul-de-sacs to discourage high-speed through traffic. Except for a very few frame homes from the pre-Fire era, most structures are "post-Fire" Victorian styles of the 1870s and 1880s. One of the houses, now Forkert's own home, defies the usual Victorian pattern books. It has a fairy-tale quality about it, with characteristics of a Swiss chalet: a wide

St. Michael's Church rose from the 1871 Chicago fire like a phoenix, creating a link with the past that nobody in the Old Town Triangle can ignore. Every day its bells remind them who they are and where they are.

overhanging veranda supported by curved brackets, openwork above the windows, and carved wooden spindle railings flanking the broad stairway leading to the second-floor front door. It was built in 1874 by a brewer who fled Germany along with his compatriots after an unsuccessful attempt to gain power for the middle classes during the aborted 1848 revolution against the nobility. The newest owner has restored the home from what was "an old wreck" during the earlier part of this century to a handsome, authentic Victorian-era home.

Just down the street is another page from the book of American architecture, five brick row houses designed by Louis Sullivan and built in 1885. Although termed "simplified Queen Anne," these chaste façades speak pure Sullivan in intricate terra-cotta ornamentation. At the time of the Victory gardens, these row houses were flophouses, containing thirty-six families. Today each is a single-family home, a product of a determined neighborhood and a reawakened sense of historic value.

Our main strength is the young people moving in.

Maurice Forkert is one of that rare breed: the preservationist of the 1940s. He has saved old homes for urban living when it was not fashionable to do so. Today, he and his contemporaries are in the unique position of viewing their activities and their neighborhood's restoration not from the eyes of the newly christened back-to-the-city movement, but from the eyes of the old warriors who had their back-to-the-city experience long before many of the present old-house savers were born. They have had their victory. They have lived long in a gradually restoring neighborhood. So what can they tell the neophyte preservationist about the future of old neighborhoods?

Forkert says that the payoff question is what will happen to his Old Town Triangle when the old-timers die out or retire. And he feels that the answer is already here. The amazing thing is that he is seeing the development of a whole new generation that is again returning to the city, returning to the Triangle. The neighborhood's

Chicago architect Louis Sullivan was one of the first to simplify the Victorian elaboration of structures. His 1885 brick row houses became "modern" while still keeping some details of terra-cotta ornamentation. This foreshadowed his revolutionary architectural innovations which were to change architecture around the world.

main strength today is no longer the old people, but the young people who are moving in from the suburbs. The child of the suburbanite has expanded his and her horizons, perceiving the quality of life that can only be found in the bustle of the city.

Here the opera, the symphony, the art institute, the museums, are only fifteen minutes away—by bus. A total of six bus lines can speed you into the city center from the Lincoln Park area. Forkert himself hasn't driven his car into the city for work or recreation for twenty years. He and his wife go by bus.

Even when the question of city crime comes up, Forkert replies that in his experience and in statistical examples, crime is becoming no more of a problem in the city than it is in the suburbs.

Nineteenth-century townhouses are probably the most urban of residential structures. These carved doors, graced with cherubs, were brought from Europe to advertise the builder's pride in his Lincoln Park home.

There is always some neighborhood activity going on here, including one of the oldest annual art fairs in the country. People know their neighbors, so every street has many eyes watching over the community. He echoes a phrase heard in many successful preservation neighborhoods around the nation, "People care about each other here."

Successful preservation demands an absence of exploitation.

Another lesson the old-timers of Lincoln Park can teach young preservationists is to beware of the entrepreneurs who see the exploitation pos-

sibilities in turning "Old Towns" into honky-tonks. Just to the west of the Lincoln Park area runs Wells Street, a street of formerly handsome old Victorian homes and commercial buildings.

About fifteen years ago, as the Lincoln Park residents were first achieving restoration success in their area, other people began restoring buildings along Wells Street both for residential and commercial use. But as the street grew more attractive and visitors came to admire the buildings, other more money-minded people began to see the exploitation possibilities of this increasingly busy street. Eventually, what began as a gradual rehabilitation of the buildings for a more traditional residential-oriented usage became a bizarrer tansformation of several blocks of the street.

There are times when good architecture loses to exploitation. This is one of them. The "Old Town" on Wells Street should not be confused with Maurice Forkert's nearby Old Town Triangle neighborhood.

Because of a lack of historic zoning, design control, and use control, these several blocks of jazzed-up Victorian buildings began to draw what a disgusted Lincoln Park resident called "the suburban mink-manure trade" for a series of porno shops, skin flicks, and assorted garish bars. One of the finest old Victorian homes was painted nightmare colors and became a "haunted house" disco.

To add insult to injury, the new breed of proprietors on this section of Wells Street appropriated the name "Old Town" from their Old Town Triangle neighbors. But not surprisingly, the throngs of people who originally came to view the newly restored buildings and to spend money in the more neighborhood-oriented cafes and shops are not returning to see the old houses in their new bawdy dress. The proprietors cannot understand why their "Old Town" gimmick is no longer working, now that Carpenter Gothic gingerbread and Queen Anne stained glass are covered over with sex signs and Day-Glo paint. The Lincoln Park neighbors only hope that this, too, will pass. The sturdy old buildings have survived fire and depression. Maybe they can survive an advanced case of exploitation as well.

Pullman is an island of stability surrounded by a sea of change.

As you drive south from Chicago's Loop on Highway 90, a series of low-income high-rises stand between Lake Michigan and the freeway like gigantic rocket launching pads. They were built only a few years ago as the ultimate answer in solving a city's housing problems, yet have only succeeded in causing more problems of vandalism, crime, and speedy deterioration. Yet, just across the freeway is another experiment in low-cost housing which began in 1880 and is working as well today as it did almost one hundred years ago.

George M. Pullman built Chicago's first planned industrial community to house the workers of his Pullman Palace Car Company. The community of Queen Anne-style brick homes and rowhouses made from Lake Michigan mud has survived practically intact through wars, depres-

sions, and block-busting while communities all around it were succumbing to "white flight," deterioration, and urban renewal.

The reasons why this predominantly blue-collar community survived may be instructive to other communities that wish to survive in an ever-changing world.

Pullman had an initial asset because it was conceived by a man of vision and executed by an architect (Solon S. Beman) who had sensitivity to a small residential community's needs. In 1880, when few capitalists were interested in providing amenities for their employees, George Pullman was wise enough to know that to get and keep good workers one had to offer them a better quality of life than one's competitors. Tree-lined streets were laid out, attractive Victorian-style homes were built for the company managers, comfortable townhouses for the married workers and their families, and even rooming houses for the bachelor workers. Every room in every home had a window with an outdoor view. Churches, parks, even a grand hotel and market were designed for the self-contained community of some eight hundred homes.

In addition, employment has continued to be available, both in the Pullman factory and in other nearby industrial firms. But the strongest element in the stability of this community has been the determination of the original residents to grow roots and hold on in spite of everything. The Polish and Italian craftsmen established a community in this 1880's "instant town." Their children stayed, and their children's children. Even in the bad old days of the 1950s and 60s, when the flight to the suburbs hit urban centers all over the nation like a plague, most of the Pullman residents remained where they were born. Even when the community next to them, Roseland, changed within eighteen months in the early 1970s from 95 per cent middle-income white to 90 per cent poorer black residents, Pullman remained stable, although a little more shabby than before.

The greatest blow of all was in the early 1960s when the city of Chicago published an urban renewal plan which showed the entire community of Pullman replaced by a proposed industrial park. As in most remaining historic areas, this

David Gillespie, executive director of the Historic Pullman Foundation, says that one gauge of restoration activity is the amount of scaffolding around a building. His Hotel Florence appears to be the winner as it nears restoration as a multi-use faculty for Pullman residents and visitors.

woke up the community to the fact that if they were to survive, they had to get organized. They formed the Pullman Civic Organization for political activities and the Historic Pullman Foundation for active restoration and re-use of the deteriorated homes and commercial buildings. When there was a public referendum for the establishment of the area as a City Landmark District, of the 1,300 eligible voters, 720 residents voted yea with only one person voting against the ordinance.

People soon learn that most modern tract houses are candidates for tomorrow's slums.

The Historic Pullman Foundation has developed an inventory of 780 historic and architecturally important structures and has established a set of community goals and objectives which include an evaluation of the practical re-use potential for several important nonresidential structures in the community. Foundation director David Gillespie is especially proud of the present restoration of the Hotel Florence for local community use as meeting place, hotel, restaurant, and activity center. Next will be the restoration of the Market Hall complex. Then the profits from these projects will be used to seed a revolving fund to help local residents restore their homes and to make grants for restoration and façade easement programs.

Home ownership has increased dramatically since earlier residents of Pullman are now returning. These row houses are being restored by mostly blue-collar residents who have learned that old houses can be better than anything the suburban developers can offer.

The architecture of Historic Pullman holds many surprises, like this hand-carved wall detail. It is an example of how some old houses may have been designed for the lower-income working family, but they were definitely not "low class."

In the last five years, owner-occupancy in the community has increased from 60 per cent to 80 per cent. An especially interesting statistic is that 95 per cent of the residents continue to be blue-collar, with only 5 per cent white-collar professionals. Many of the new residents are either the children of former residents or the original residents who fled to the suburbs and then discovered that suburban tract houses could not compete with the stability of the old houses and friends of Pullman.

Gillespie feels that Pullman is proving to be one of the most exciting preservation projects in the Midwest, if not the nation. It is a community of old houses and old families that has held onto its original residents while restoring its structures and quality of life. New residents are welcomed, but original residents have first chance at restoration opportunities. Even the city fathers in uptown Chicago have been convinced that Pullman is here to stay, and city funds are restoring George Pullman's park and helping to repair the hotel.

The community may still be relatively "low income" but it is not low class. It is also not low in its residents' courage and determination, and in their ability to come up with creative solutions to complex revitalization problems.

You Can Go Home Again: Marshall

Marshall, Michigan, is one of the finest naturally preserved small towns in America. It is what every preservationist sees in his mind's eye as he scrapes generations of paint off walls, attends endless neighborhood meetings, and makes impassioned speeches about improving a community's "quality of life."

And at a time when almost every other small town in America is trying to look like every other by covering Victorian-style Main Streets with plastic store fronts and fast-food architecture, when every city is trying to "renew" itself by bringing either suburban split-level living to its neighborhoods or poured concrete high-rises to its downtown, Marshall has dared to be different. It is perfectly content to look and be the way it always has, a unique, beautifully maintained twentieth-century town with nineteenth-century architecture, values, and quality of life.

It was a bustling community of 7,000 people back in 1847 when it lost out to Lansing in the competition to become the capitol city of Michigan. Today it is a bustling community of 7,500 which somehow has survived the rush to the twentieth-century practically intact. More than 1,200 exquisitely detailed homes; Italianate, Greek Revival, Gothic Revival, Queen Anne, and every nineteenth-century architecturally styled home in between, glow in pastel colors under giant maple trees like some living exhibition of Currier & Ives prints.

What happened here? What great miracle of common sense could have occurred here as the rest of the country was destroying itself under the enthusiastic urgings of chambers of commerce, get-rich-quick developers, and urban planners?

The answer seems to lie in a fateful combination of geography, extraordinary people, and luck. There were, of course, dreamers of wealth and fame who lived in Marshall, too, as some of the grand eccentricities of the homes suggest. In fact, the town was settled by an elite of New England doctors, lawyers, educators, and capitalists who had big dreams for Marshall from the beginning. They even built a governer's mansion on speculation and laid out imposing avenues for the dreamed-of government complex on a little rise of land they named Capitol Hill. But their efforts were defeated by one vote.

Yet their enthusiasm continued as everyone expected Marshall to become the Midwest's railroad center. In 1863, the Brotherhood of the Footboard was formed; it later evolved into the powerful Brotherhood of Locomotive Engineers. But they, and the Michigan Central Railroad yards, moved to Jackson in the 1870s. Finally, even Marshall's booming patent medicine business lost out to the Pure Food and Drug Act. In

This 1887 modified Queen Anne-style residence was built by the president of the Marshall Folding Bathtub Company. It has been beautifully restored by the Norman D. Kinneys. (Photo courtesy Marshall Historical Society.)

the meantime, the rush of immigrants passed the little town by, opting for the nearby magnets of Chicago and Detroit.

Bad luck? Or how could Marshall have been so fortunate?

There always has been a certain social integrity here as well as architectural integrity.

The people of Marshall have seemed to keep an unshaken confidence in themselves and their town. In spite of the many early failed hopes,

residents have included a governor, a U. S. Council to the Hawaiian Islands, and assorted inventors and millionaires such as the man who invented the folding bathtub. Most came back to live in Marshall after their brief jousts with fame, and some, like Harold C. Brooks, never left.

Mr. Brooks took over his parents' rupture-appliance business in 1912. With the wry motto: "Brooks supports the world—and we'll never let it down," he expanded the second-story storefront operation into a world-wide business. Once mayor of the town, he has been its benefactor for over fifty years.

The Honolulu House was built in 1860 by Judge Abner Pratt, a former U. S. Consul to the Sandwich Islands. Saved from deterioration by Harold Brooks, it is now a public museum and headquarters of the Marshall Historical Society. (Photo courtesy of Marshall Historical Society.)

If a fine old house was threatened with deterioration or abandonment, he would buy it and hold on to it until he found an owner interested in restoration and preservation. He has owned, at one time or another, well over a dozen key homes in Marshall. For example, he held the Honolulu House, built by the past U. S. Council to remind him of his past glories and now called "Marshall's Crown Jewel," for eleven years until the Marshall Historical Society was able to purchase it from him.

A pioneer of adaptive use of old structures, Mr. Brooks encouraged the city to transform an 1857 livery stable and auto garage into a handsome Town Hall. When asked how Brooks was able to sell the idea to the citizens, a friend replied, "It was very simple. He paid 80 per cent of the cost himself." Displeased with the mundane design of a new U. S. Post Office the government wished to build, Brooks made a deal to provide the architect and materials if the government would pay for the labor.

But Harold Brooks is not unique in Marshall. Many other citizens, in less spectacular ways, have shown their appreciation and respect for the integrity of their community.

Nobody would ever move away from here, or if they did, they always come back.

Creighton Sherman was born in Marshall fifty-two years ago, went away to college to become a landscape architect and urban planner, and then came back home to sell shoes and restore old houses. He says that once you live here you just sort of take it for granted and love it and feel comfortable here. You like it so well that you want it to stay looking nice. It's not that people in Marshall have less ambition than people in other towns and cities. It's just that if they have any sense, they know that no other place can make you feel so satisfied and good as do the old houses and shady streets of Marshall.

Sherman and his wife, Becky, have raised four children and fixed up several houses in town. Even though they don't have the money of a Brooks, they feel about shabby houses as one does about a neglected kitten. It just seems the thing to do to take it in, clean it up, and see if you can find a good owner for it. It's not so much one's civic duty as a moral obligation.

Part of the reason may be because of the feeling of stability and continuity one gets from living in an old house. As Becky explains, "It's been

In the Sherman's dining room, the portrait over the fireplace is of Mary Haskell, one of the first infants to be born in the new Marshall community.

around a lot longer than you have and you figure it will stay around a lot longer after you're gone. As people get older and less able to take care of the house, they move out and a younger generation comes in and puts their love in it, and then they go on, and the next generation takes over. I'm not against new houses. They're nice to visit, but I wouldn't want to live in one."

You are attracted by the architecture, then decide to stay when you meet the people.

This town also seems to draw its strength from new people who move here because they respect the same values as the old-timers, including the architecture. One of Marshall's most fortunate aspects is that it has several stable industries which also seem to appreciate and respect Marshall's clean and historic atmosphere, such as the

Creighton and Becky Sherman stand on the side porch of their 1844 home. Enlarged in 1870 to Italianate style, it is a comfortable, personal home.

home offices of the Eaton Corporation's Fluid Power Division and State Farm Insurance. Natives and outsiders can afford to stay because there are good jobs available. There is no problem for the companies to convince bright junior executives to move to Marshall. The only problem is that once an employee is transferred from another part of the country, it is difficult to make him and his family leave for another assignment.

John Collins is one of the transplants to Marshall, leaving the sophistication of Boston to become Director of Publicity for the Eaton Corporation. He also became president of the Marshall Historical Society and enthusiastic promoter and protector of the special Marshall quality of life. Recently, he was elected president of the Historical Society of Michigan. Every successful community in the process of preservation has a John Collins if they are lucky. He, or she, is the person who contributes an inordinate amount of time and energy for the benefit of the community, articulating its causes, demanding and receiving an equal amount of time and energy from friends and neighbors who never dreamed they could volunteer so much time or have so much fun "doing good."

John is a great believer in diversity, to achieve and keep that hazy goal of quality of life. The combination of long-time residents with their

John Collins, the ultimate preservation publicity man, displays another of his Home Tour creations. Few people work harder, and few have more fun, than does former Marshall Historical Society president Collins.

Lines of visitors from hundreds of miles away stand patiently, in order to experience a moment of history each year during the Marshall Historic Home Tour. (Courtesy Marshall Historical Society.)

generations-long roots in the past and new people from around the world who are drawn here from different backgrounds creates a unique climate for both stability and cultural growth. One can go to a party in Marshall and meet people from Boston, Los Angeles, London. Yet there is little conflict between local and nonlocal people because a primary interest—the houses—continues to unite both. A greater sense of neighborliness seems to develop when diverse people are involved in a community, when they have a cause to believe in, when they have something to be proud of. The traditional negative effects of "parochialism" are erased, leaving a universal concern for a unique sense of place which bursts the bounds of petty narrowness toward a greater

Every year, with cannons booming and rifles cracking, men in blue and gray uniforms fight the Battle of Capitol Hill. Civil War enthusiasts gather in Marshall to play at this noisy ballet of heroism before crowds of thousands. It makes no difference that there never was a historic battle here to commemorate. It makes no difference that no one knows how each year's battle will end. It is a celebration of a heritage of valor and nostalgia that has ceased to draw blood yet continues to draw clouds of glory. (Photo courtesy Marshall Historical Society.)

appreciation of the old, the humane, the renewal of a sense of identity and relatedness in everyone.

One of the unifying causes in which all of Marshall gets involved is the annual home tour. In the fourteenth annual tour of 1977, over thirty-five Marshall organizations and over 1,600 volunteers were embroiled in the mind-boggling logistics of responsibilities for fourteen homes and public buildings on tour, as well as orchestrating the Grand Old-fashioned Parade; an Arts and Crafts Fair; an Antiques Show; an Old-fashioned Band Concert; a Civil War Re-enactment: "Battle of Capitol Hill"; and many more events. Eight thousand people paid to take the tour and thousands more came to see the other events—all through the efforts of a town with a total population of 7,500.

Many visitors compliment John and his friends on their courage in opening their homes to all those strangers. But he reflects that house-tour visitors must be especially nice types because not one household item has been stolen in the fourteen years of Marshall's tours. He feels that it is the visitors who drive two hundred miles and more, and then stand in line for an hour or more, who should be complimented for their courage.

The annual home tour is a great tonic for the community, too. In the preceding weeks, every-

one cleans up and paints up their property, even if their homes are not on tour. Although some scoff at all the frivolity and catering to strangers, almost everyone takes a secret pride in it. Neglected porches suddenly appear with a coat of

Although only a dozen or so homes are on tour each year, every homeowner feels part of the great event. Not surprisingly, everybody's annual fix-up time seems to coincide just before the home tour begins. (Courtesy Marshall Historical Society.)

paint. Long neglected gardens often spruce up overnight as tour day approaches.

The children benefit most from Marshall's celebration of civic pride and history. They are schooled in the pride of place and heritage by one of the nation's few complete school curriculums on local history and architecture. Every student must write a class paper about what he or she likes about Marshall before graduating from high school. And each year before the formal opening of the house tour, the school children are given a special tour of the houses.

We weren't quite brave enough to live downtown in a big city, but Marshall's just right.

Many people come to see the houses on the annual tour, and then come back to stay. Mike Kinter and his wife and children decided to move to Marshall two years ago after a friend of his bought a home here. It reminded him of the small town where he was born. It seemed a little safer here, with less of the risks he feels that big city "pioneers" must face.

A teacher, Kinter decided to also change his

Mike Kinter—a teacher turned carpenter, shopkeeper, restorationist—works in his shop. It sure is better than a nine-to-five job, he says. You're working for yourself, and all the problems, and rewards, are your own.

profession when he made the move. He is now rehabilitating an old store for a gift shop. He is one of the first, along the town's main street, to tear off the 1950s "modernizations" on the building façade and is restoring it to its original Victorian style. He is also working on his Queen Anne-style home, feeling that the complete investment he is making in time and money is secure in a town which has so much respect for its old buildings.

After many years of searching, he finally has an ideal setting for his collection of music boxes and mechanical musical devices. To the rear of the store will be a 1920s theater organ built into the room, ready to celebrate special occasions and for any organ aficionado who comes into town. His store will complement the one being restored just down the street by one of the nation's most respected magicians. For people of imagination and wit, Marshall seems to have a special attraction.

None of us would ever dream this would happen, and it's kind of scary.

There is always the problem of a community becoming too attractive. Most residents who are proud of their homes and their accomplishments are pleased to show others their source of pride. But the growth of outside interest in Marshall has become extraordinary in recent years. Television crews and journalists are coming to point cameras and scribble in increasing numbers. Busloads of tourists from as far away as Delaware are arriving, sometimes several buses a day, to peer and point excitedly from tinted windows.

Sue Collins, wife of John, is in charge of a group of Marshall Historical Society volunteers who ride the scheduled buses, telling about the town and its houses. But more and more buses are coming each day, clogging the streets as well as the volunteer's schedules until even these gracious volunteers wonder just how hospitable one can be.

Maybe it is because of the American Bicentennial. Maybe it is because of the excellent publicity efforts of John Collins and his associates. Maybe it is just because of a growing national awareness of just how much of the good we have thrown away with the bad for the sake of "progress." But somehow to many people, Marshall, Michigan, has become a symbol of a life which once was but never can be again for many other cities and towns.

People here seem a little nicer. The pace of life seems a little slower and more comfortable. People go home for lunch and do a little gardening before going back to work. The architecture is so beautiful that it takes your breath away. The rich and middle income live in big old houses and the poor and lower middle income live in little old houses. But every house is clean, cared for, a work of art. And the people living inside them express a sense of pride, a self-consciousness of place.

The people from Detroit and Cleveland and Chicago come in autos and buses to press their faces against the window glass and marvel at the sights from another time. Then they get back on Freeway 94 and drive home, wondering why their neighborhood couldn't be like that, wondering if they should quit their jobs· and all their conceptions of twentieth-century success and move to Marshall.

The folks in Marshall clean up after the crowds and the buses, pleased that so many people appreciate the same things they do. The old houses continue to be bought and sold and fixed up at a brisk but reasonable pace as people die or are transferred to Kansas City. There is talk about one of the giant Detroit auto firms buying up two thousand acres just outside of town. Contrary to the business boosterism of most towns, people here pray it isn't so.

Maybe the one thing folks in Marshall have learned which could revolutionize every city and town in America is this: New is not necessarily better. Big is not necessarily best. The classic chamber-of-commerce chant of the more industry, the more jobs, the more happiness is a siren's song which can destroy a community.

Knowing who you are and where you come from. Learning to value what you have instead of worrying about how to get something else. Using something until it wears out and then fixing it up for someone else to use. Maybe this kind of philosophy won't make you the size of Detroit or as rich as Houston. But maybe that's all right, too.

The front porches of Marshall are the best expressions of why people have love affairs with old houses. Built in 1853, the porch of this Italian Villa says "welcome" in a timeless and universal language.

A City Saved in Spite of Itself: Portland

The decline and rise of Portland, Maine, is not unique. The dynamics which are causing the restoration of this coastal seaport town on the rocky shores of Casco Bay have been repeated in many American cities. But the little ironies of the preservation process here are so clearly symbolic that they hold a mirror up to us all.

By 1770, Portland was one of the most prosperous of the original American colonies. The wealth of its ocean and its forests was exported to the world through a dozen or more bustling finger wharfs which jutted out from the harbor front on Fore Street. It was the harbor which provided the lifeblood of the city and the stimulus for the construction of grand Federal and Greek Revival-style houses on the hillsides above the activity of the waterfront.

But the familiar pattern of deterioration began, with the wealthier citizens moving farther away from the life-giving center of town, out to the Western Promenade and beyond. Then shipping activity moved southward to Boston and Baltimore. After World War II, the last great source of sea-gained revenue, the shipyard, also closed. The city seemed to lose its confidence. Like so many cities across the nation, it began to commit suicide by destroying itself in the name of urban renewal.

On a sunny August day in 1961, the city of Portland enacted a singular drama of self-destruction which was so symbolic of the postwar urban renewal era that it lives today as a rallying point for preservationists everywhere. To make way for a strip shopping center, the massive stone Châteauesque-style Portland Union Station was demolished. Although few people were there to see the building fall, a photographer, Donald E. Johnson, was. His photo of the gigantic clock tower of the railroad station, with its ornamental stonework at the tower's peak just beginning to topple as the intricate jigsaw puzzle of Maine granite blocks below it collapses in a sea of rubble, has become a silent, visual scream against wanton demolition.

Yet, the greatest irony of all is that the shopping center which replaced this priceless landmark, which a Portland resident describes as the most classically atrocious, ugly strip commercial complex that you could conjure up in your imagination, has lost most of its tenants and for several years has been standing almost vacant. Every square foot of its retail space could have fit comfortably within the station. But there was no thought to the re-use alternative back in 1961, no vision of it at all among the busy minds of the business-boosting members of the chamber of commerce and the city council.

A city has to believe in itself.

The destruction of the Portland Union Station was the call to action for city preservationists. It remains a symbol for all of us to remember. (Photo courtesy Portland *Evening Express* and Donald Johnson.)

The demolition of the Union Station was the Portland preservationist's call to action, a rude awakening for a city's citizens who placed too much faith in their democratically elected representatives' ability to always make the right decisions. Followed by the demolition of a magnificent nineteenth-century federal post office, Greater Portland Landmarks, Inc., was formed.

A few people, at the risk of being labeled ding-bats and antibusiness, began speaking out against the destruction of old buildings. A few historic buildings were given to the small group, some to be moved away from the pathways of progress (freeways and parking lots). These were secured for new owners who agreed to restore and protect them. From the sale of the houses, a small revolving fund was established for further preservation efforts. As each succeeding threatened home was saved and resold, the new owner signed a protective covenant which guaranteed that the exterior of the building would be authentically restored and continue to be preserved in the future.

Today, Greater Portland Landmarks, Inc., has grown to almost a thousand members in this city of sixty thousand. Its present director, Joel Russ, has finally been able to move a Historic District ordinance through the labyrinth of city government and out to the overwhelming support of a series of city-wide neighborhood meetings. It has taken ten years and nine drafts of the ordinance to steer it past the new construction-oriented battlements of successively more receptive city council members.

The citizens of Portland are beginning to believe in the city again, beginning to understand the values of the buildings which have been standing since the Revolutionary and Civil wars. They are also beginning to understand that if something needs doing, you had better do it yourself.

There has been no single driving force or governmental edict behind the creation of the residential and commercial renaissance in Portland, although the Portland Landmarks organization helped. It was only individuals, the so-called amateurs, doing their own thing which caused Portland to restore itself. And for some miraculous reason, the many little efforts have all come together.

Portland's road to recovery began after the shock of the destruction of the Union Station when the sons and daughters of suburbanites began moving back to the city. In addition, young people from Dallas and St. Louis and other Midwestern cities began to heed the call of the Eastern seaboard. But instead of Boston or New York or Baltimore, they came to the smaller seacoast cities where opportunities seemed greater and population pressures less.

One such couple was Pam and Peter Plum, who moved from St. Louis in 1969. They wanted to live in the city, to live in an old house. Their search ended when they purchased an 1835 Greek Revival townhouse on Park Street Row. Pam believes that the charm of the house and the

Pam Plumb and her son wait at the front door of their 1835 Park Street Row townhouse. Still in much of its original condition, the Greek Revival-style home boasts a full-size pipe organ on its second floor.

urban environment have permanently addicted them to living in town.

Peter can walk to his law office in the Old Port Exchange commercial area just down the hill. Their two children can walk to school and to activities at the Y. Pam can do almost all her errands by walking. They need only one car, which mostly stays in the garage. They use their feet, and it has made a tremendous difference in their lives where all the previous hours spent in commuting have been placed back in their lives like a gift, to be used for doing anything they wish.

> *The old houses were a gravy train for slum-lords.*

Pam Plum is now president of Greater Portland Landmarks, Inc., and even she is surprised by the rapid improvement in the neighborhoods. Almost every building on her block has been rehabilitated, either by the present owner or new and younger owners. Many of the old houses in the surrounding neighborhoods were previously carved up into fifteen or more apartments by absentee owners, some of whom could be rightfully given the title "slumlord."

The classic forces of slumlordism seem to operate in a very specific manner. He discards most of the single-family interior amenities of a building, puts lots of little rental units in it, then takes all the money out of it until it falls down. By that time, it is already amortized; he has written it off, and he walks away from it. He is admired for being a smart businessman, while the city taxpayers and the neighborhood residents wonder why their once beautiful community has slowly become a "slum."

Yet there are now new forces at play which are slowly but surely putting the slumlord out of business. The values are changing. And it is the small resident developer, the person still interested in making a profit, but also interested in the history and architecture of the building, who is beginning to help "unslum" neighborhoods. Just as a new attitude about a building can change the perceived value of that building and its surrounding neighborhood, so too can the building change the person involved in restoring it.

The youngest member of the Plumb family earns his own "sweat equity" by sanding an antique chest of drawers.

Thomas Thomsen is a good example of how an old house can change a person's life. He graduated from college with a degree in public administration and government, then for six years worked for the State Department in Washington, D.C. Today he is a carpenter and an old-house restoration contractor. He has rehabilitated an 1803 Federal-style house in Portland and another 1832 house, mostly with his own hands.

People, he says, used to feel so bound to a job or to a place that they didn't have the imagination or the courage to do what they really wanted to do. But most of the new people who are moving to Portland are making a conscious decision to first find the living environment that they really prefer. Only after they find that, will they then try to see what they can find for employment, which is often something entirely different from what they first imagined.

Thomas Thomsen, former U. S. State Department official and now master carpenter and old-home restorer, has transformed a neglected slum (left) into a handsome restored early Federal-style house (right). (Left photo courtesy Greater Portland Landmarks, Inc.)

He likes what he is doing now. The old buildings give him a chance to create living spaces that are unusual. They aren't just the usual sheet-rocked rectangles with aluminum windows. He pointed proudly to the purloined rafters in his 1832 house, a huge hand-carved roof beam with rough-hewn rafters laid on top of it. Whether it is a friend or a building, you've got to take care of it, he says.

Thomsen has had to rebuild almost everything in the house and has spent more money than he should. But he doesn't want a cheap building, a building that doesn't express its basic integrity. So he tries to bring out the personality each structure has, sculpting a deteriorated house like a block of marble, allowing the beams and joists to speak to him, waiting for the original floor plan and its historic character to speak to him.

The Old Port Exchange is the single most exciting area of the city.

Henry Willette was a city planner and chief landscape architect for the city of Portland. For nine years he tried to convince the city decision-makers that one of their chief assets was the deteriorated, almost completely abandoned waterfront district. While most people in city government hoped for demolition of the blocks of old brick commercial buildings, Willette saw the buildings as the most potentially attractive amenities of downtown. He had studied European planning and architectural techniques and was well aware of the value hidden behind the grimy nineteenth-century three- and four-story buildings.

But his superiors thought they knew better. Four-story buildings were selling for as little as $800 along the waterfront. Entire floors of the buildings could be rented for a few dollars a month, provided the owner could find anyone crazy enough to want the space. The director of the city's urban renewal department was reported to have said that he once took his family "down there a while ago and it was awful. Crossing Commercial Street was a terror. I finally scooped up the kids and ran."

Henry Willette, with the help of architect Walter Cantwell, has created a relaxed and spacious apartment on the fourth floor of his 1866 Italianate commercial building. Much of the woodwork was salvaged from other buildings.

Nobody believed in the Old Port Exchange, except Willette. So in 1966 he quit his job and began to purchase what eventually totaled seventeen of the Civil War-era buildings. His former associates laughed. He had little money, but the buildings were so ridiculously cheap that by renting spaces for $5.00 a week and opening up a candle shop for extra cash flow, he was able to keep the structures from the wrecking ball. No bank would finance his renovation, so he did almost everything by himself and talked potential tenants into rehabilitating their own spaces.

Then other individuals became interested in the area. A plating and giftware foundry moved in. Two men opened the Old Port Tavern steak house in an abandoned cellar of a warehouse. It was an immediate success, helping to provide evening traffic in the area. Its success brought in the Gas Light Restaurant, featuring French cuisine, which opened in an old Board of Trade building.

In less than ten years, a run-down collection of commercial buildings, warehouses, and slum apartments has become the most exciting, most desirable part of the city. This entire process is a classic monument to individual small entrepreneurship and sweat equity, practically completely bypassing any federal urban renewal spending or city government involvement. In fact, the renovation of the Old Port Exchange, which covers a significant part of the downtown landholdings, was well advanced before the city officials fully realized what was happening right under their very noses. By then, Willette's former coworkers weren't laughing at him anymore.

Mixed use is the secret to success.

Today the buildings in the Old Port Exchange command higher rental rates than do most of the office buildings in Portland's center city where millions of dollars have been spent for urban renewal. Part of the reason for the success of the restored area is a complementary mixed use within the buildings: shops in the basement and on the first floor, offices on the second, and apartments on the third and fourth floors.

The recently vacant and ignored commercial slum has become a multi-use, twenty-four-hour-a-day, seven-day-a-week neighborhood. The combination of office workers, shopkeepers, customers, restaurant and theater clients, as well as full-time residents, keeps the streets active and colorful every hour of the day. This area, which had the highest crime rate in the city, now has the lowest. This former debit for the city has now more than quadrupled its tax flow to city coffers. And now, there also seems to be a solid turnaround in the city's population statistics, with people moving back to the restored houses on the hills above and to the Old Port Exchange on the waterfront.

These dozen or so blocks of tightly packed buildings between the Fore River and the center city have become one of the more authentic "old towns" in the nation, a sensitive and practical re-use of the past which has become a logical continuity to the future. Young people with young ideas, exciting shops and commercial ventures, seem to make everything work. The new businesses exist cheek by jowl with businesses and pubs which have survived for generations. Even the nationally televised "Today" show came to see the revitalization of Portland, forcing the still unbelieving mayor to acknowledge that there indeed seemed to be restoration activity going on in his city. Yet, not too long ago, the Old Port Exchange property owners had to pay the city's share of matching federal funds to make sidewalk improvement in their area. But, recently, even the astute city officials are beginning to see the benefits of urban restoration and are acknowledging that the Old Port Exchange may after all be here to stay.

Everybody pitches in to make the place a success.

Hank Willette's economic philosophy may be termed "pragmatic preservation." Because no one else could see the value of the old buildings, he was able to secure them for a small amount of money (his own), a lot of personal sweat equity, and then he found tenants who had the same dream and the same energy he had who could help him finish the job.

For example, his building at 11 Exchange Street is an Italianate-style commercial structure built in 1866 and reconstructed to a Colonial Revival style in 1898 after a fire. Again burned in 1973, and subsequently boarded up, it was purchased by Willette for $5,000. He constructed shops on the first floor, craft studios and living spaces on the second and third floors, and built his own dramatic home on the fourth floor. The interior of his spacious apartment reveals a huge fireplace, Gothic arches, stained-glass windows, and antique furniture which express his inventiveness of designing unique spaces with cost-cutting salvaged materials.

Robin Whitten and her associate weave colorful fabrics in her studio workshop in Willette's 11 Exchange Building. She did her own rehabilitation of the space, designing it to fit her needs for home, workshop, and sales area.

At the very beginning of his restoration battle, he had to rent space for $5.00 a week. By 1977, he was able to rent unimproved space for $125 per month for a three years' lease if the tenants themselves would do the restoration of their space. Willette keeps control of the quality of rehabilitation by helping the tenant draw up the rehab plans and by choosing the materials. Also, by letting the tenant do his or her own renovation, he gets a different kind of tenant who is committed to the building and to the community on a long-term basis. Owner and tenants work co-operatively for the same dream, sharing the costs in order to achieve it.

Transforming buildings into a community.

David Schurman is another developer of old buildings in the Old Port Exchange who is pushing the restoration concept into even more interesting realms. He has combined seven old commercial buildings into a multi-use complex called "The Exchange." Directly across from Willette's 11 Exchange Street, this interesting streetscape of nineteenth-century buildings is being physically joined together, keeping the exterior storefronts with all their architectural authenticity, but revolutionizing the entire 55,000 square feet of in-

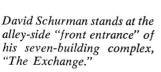

David Schurman stands at the alley-side "front entrance" of his seven-building complex, "The Exchange."

The real front entrance of "The Exchange." The entire façade of the street has been restored to enhance the amazing architectural integrity and continuity of the Old Port Exchange area.

terior space on five levels into a fluid and modern complex of shops, offices, studios, restaurants, and apartments.

Schurman is an architect who gained his preservation re-use experience working in Boston on such projects as the Inland Commercial Wharf. And he has learned that a viable commercial restoration needs the stability of a classical mixed neighborhood. The involvement of a building's tenants, as well as the interest of prospective customers for the commercial parts of the project, are enhanced when they see themselves as part of a larger, more complex identity.

Schurman, like Willette, uses tenant sweat equity to help keep rents lower. And he has created a sense of interior "transparency" by linking the buildings together, balancing the structures' spaces and uses so they are about 40 per cent commercial, 40 per cent residential, and 20 per cent office. The basement and first floor are opened to form a kind of multi-use atrium. Arched openings between the buildings lead the eye all through the complexes' 140-foot length. "The Exchange" even has two "front entrances" because Schurman has transformed the alley into another inviting street, making the grand old structures open and welcome to the entire city.

A new tenant of "The Exchange" earns his share of "sweat equity" as he rehabilitates his own residence and studio.

You can almost see forever through the seven buildings and 140 feet of "The Exchange." Archways lead the eye to make this retail/office/residential complex "transparent."

The Old Port Exchange is a place for people every hour of the day. Yet, a few years ago, the city's urban renewal director "scooped up the kids and ran" from this area.

After a quarter century of vacancy, this 1871 Italianate-style building in the Old Port Exchange can once again display one of the most beautiful stairways in America.

Deteriorated downtowns can learn much from Portland, both by looking at the renewed Federal-style homes on the hills and the transformed commercial buildings of the Old Port Exchange on the waterfront below. The lessons express good old Yankee ingenuity at its best, as well as the kind of capitalism and hard work only a Ben Franklin could surpass. Nowhere is the American melting pot of democracy better displayed as young and old, singles and families, carpenters, musicians, former planners, lawyers, artists, and architects all make the ultimate personal commitment to save old buildings as they decide what they want to do with the rest of their lives.

The Quiet Revolution of the Poor: New York City

The abandoned and burned-out tenements stretch for miles along garbage-strewn streets in the South Bronx. In Harlem, vacant spaces left by demolished buildings turn a city streetscape into a gap-toothed smile of despair. The children who are forced to live in East River high-rise ghettos vent their rage in spray-can graffiti which has turned the walls of New York City into a new art form of social protest.

New York City, Fun City, has become a caricature of everything that is wrong with the urban environment; a government on the verge of bankruptcy, streets rife with crime, grime, and pessimism. Any person fleeing to any suburb need only point to the rot in the "Big Apple" to feel justified in his act.

New York City has more than 150,000 abandoned dwelling units in over 12,000 buildings, and this number is growing at a rate of a thousand buildings a year. Slumlords purchase the buildings as a tax write-off, put no money in maintenance and repair, charge the poor whatever they can pay, and then when no more profit can be made, burn the structures for the insurance or simply abandon them. In just two years, firemen have fought seven thousand fires in the South Bronx alone, an average of ten each night.

Yet, ironically, New York City is also becoming the symbol of what can be right with a city and what can be the potential and promise of the urban preservation movement. Probably because of the desperate situation of its people, new experiments in preservation, conservation, and the capitalistic system are taking place here which could change the direction of New York City's decline as well as the general public's attitude toward preservation.

The middle class is coming back to the city in spite of the efforts of city government to keep them out.

Two converging forces are moving into the vacuum of incompetence and inertia which has caused the bankruptcy of America's largest city. One is the more traditional back-to-the-city efforts of middle-class professionals who are returning to the old Manhattan and Brooklyn brownstones. Built for the middle class and the wealthy during the nineteenth century, in an extraordinary range of Federal, Greek Revival, and Italianate styles, these three- and four-story brick and stone townhouses are ideal spaces for contemporary living. Sturdy, spacious, often still elegant with original leaded glass and parquet floors, they are a tremendous housing value no matter what their present condition. A recent architectural study estimated that at today's prices, it would cost $250,000 to build a similar structure,

Graffiti, the art of the dispossessed in search of an identity, in search of a place where they know who they are and why.

The streets of New York are again echoing to the footsteps of young lovers as well as middle-income families who are returning to the city.

Too many people see a city as a forest of big buildings and bad impressions without seeing the natural amenities and the people. This provides the human scale and makes the city worth coming back to.

The brownstones of New York City and Brooklyn offer classic urban living. Handsome and compact outside, yet they have a surprising large amount of space inside. (Photo courtesy Brooklyn Union Gas Company.)

excluding the "frills" of fancy glass and woodwork.

One of the earlier people who decided to move back to the Park Slope neighborhood of Brooklyn was Everett Ortner. Besides restoring his own brownstone, he also became the catalyst of the first organized restoration movement in the city. As cofounder of the Brownstone Revival Committee of New York City, he nurtured what were about ten small restoration areas in the late 1960s to over thirty vigorous neighborhoods today.

The residents of these restored streets see themselves as part of a small town, making it easier to manage their own lives as well as relating to the gigantic backdrop of the city. Each area, often each block, may boast a neighborhood association which is designed to foster self-improvement. Each has block meetings and block parties, house tours and baby-sitting pools in order to create a personal, human-scale identity.

This is especially true across the East River in Brooklyn, where the revitalized neighborhoods have fostered an annual Brownstone Fair. In 1977, about twenty thousand people came to the one-day event to talk with neighborhood association members about their communities, learn how to strip wallpaper or fix a faucet, and take tours of restored houses in such areas as Cobble Hill, Brooklyn Heights, and Lefferts Gardens.

Part of the reason why brownstoners gather together is to prove to city officials that they indeed exist. For although today a restored brownstone may sell for well over $100,000, the brownstoner often must battle indifferent lending agencies and unenthusiastic city agencies to restore the old building. Ortner and his compatriots of the Brownstone Revival Committee, which began in 1971 with seven members and now has sixteen hundred, have been battling this indifference. With a sophisticated effort of promoting their communities as well as the suburban developers promote theirs, small pockets of old-fashioned charm and serenity are developing in the many neglected areas of this gigantic city. The middle class is coming back to live in New York City, as well as to visit.

The city has to try it now. They've tried everything else.

Ahmad Towfiq is the leader of an Orthodox Muslem sect, the Masque of Islamic Brotherhood.

Ahmad Towfiq and Philip St. Georges stand in front of the latest urban homesteading project of the Mosque of Islamic Brotherhood, Inc.

While Everett Ortner represents the classic middle-income pioneering effort to return to the city by restoring mostly single-family dwellings, Towfiq represents a new kind of urban pioneer who is struggling to stay and survive in the city. Along with their neighbors in the South Bronx, Towfiq and his Central Harlem congregation of seventy families live in the notoriously worst slums in the nation. Harlem, a community of many four- and five-story walkup tenements built around the turn of the century, has been slowly deteriorating for half a century. The poor, the Black, the minority have been funneled into these streets of slumlords, abandoned buildings and hopes until the upper half of Manhattan Island is top-heavy with most of New York's two to three million Blacks and Puerto Ricans, including over a half million unemployed and many more underemployed.

Generations of Harlem residents have lived and died knowing only the life of welfare, the bare existence of the handout. Fortunes have been made by members of the majority who administer the handout programs to the minority, firmly institutionalizing the master-slave social relationship of the ghetto. The government giver is often well-meaning, but terribly inept, as is symbolized by a so-called low-income high-rise in Harlem built recently which cost $80,000 per unit, plus up to $700 per month, per family, to help subsidize the rent needed to pay for this version of welfare.

But now Ahmad Towfiq and his friends are breaking out of the welfare trap, creating their own home out of the shell of a tenement building on West 113th Street and out of the planning and sweat of their own efforts. There will be fourteen dwelling units at an average cost of $20,000 per unit. They will own and maintain their own homes.

With thousands of buildings being abandoned and the city itself perhaps going bankrupt, New York City, out of desperation, began its Sweat Equity Program which provides low-interest loans to community residents who buy abandoned buildings from the city and perform their own renovation. The homesteader then occupies and manages the buildings as co-ops, returning them to the city's decimated stock of decent, low-cost housing.

Several American cities have homesteading programs. But a unique version of this program, sponsored by the Cathedral of Saint John the Divine, is one that refutes some municipal housing experts and planners who believe that "homesteading was never meant for the poor." Thanks to the city's Sweat Equity Program, which helps provide the buildings and the financing, the Cathedral's Urban Homesteading Assistance Board (U-Hab) provides the expert assistance for the unemployed, untrained homesteader. U-Hab provides access to trained construction supervisors, architects, cost estimaters, lawyers, accountants, and others, to channel the raw energy and enthusiasm of the potential rebuilder and owner of a badly damaged building. By the fall of 1977, U-Hab had successfully completed three multiple-housing projects, twenty-six more were in con-

struction, and eleven more were in final planning
stages.

All he needed was a chance, said Towfiq.
When the city officials began to talk with him
and his coworkers like they were men instead of
"the poor," then they were able to get something
done. They weren't looking for handouts. They
were just trying to buy into the American system
of property ownership with a classic medium of
exchange, their own sweat.

And nothing is sweeter than owning your own
home, he said as he proudly attended to the hundreds of details of reconstruction among the open
beams, rolls of insulation, and piles of sawdust in
the big apartment building. It's like a miracle,
with Towfiq and his friends working there and
the sun shining in the newly rebuilt windows
which they made themselves. Soon he would be
living in his own home with his family, there
would be a coffee house open to the public on
the first floor, and there are negotiations for the
rehabilitation of another building down the street
which means more homeowners and more jobs.

---

*Those guys, they work so hard I can't be-
lieve.*

Fernando Clementi is a construction foreman
for the Renegades of Harlem, Youth Gang for the
People. This East Harlem street gang has ex-
changed its guns and drugs for hammers and saws,
trading a life of crime for one of pursuing the
middle-class American values of hard work and

*The Renegades of Harlem, Youth Gang for the Peo-
ple, are now in the rehabilitation business. City officials are impressed with the quality of their work
and their enthusiasm as careful craftsmen.*

*Sweat equity is what they call
it, and sweat is what they
do. Everybody in Harlem
watches as the building becomes beautiful through the
work of its urban homesteaders.*

property ownership. Clementi, one of the few professional craftsmen who works with this gang of former hoodlums to rehabilitate several impossibly deteriorated buildings, is continually amazed at his coworkers' growing professional abilities in the building of walls and the laying of floors.

If these last statements sound too melodramatic, if not highly unlikely to the reader, you aren't alone. Many city officials and bankers still won't believe it either, even as these urban homesteading projects are visably working, and as the former junkies, criminals, and chronically unemployed are now restoring these buildings, maintaining them, and paying their mortgages. It is as if the poor wore some kind of stigmata to declare them physically and morally incapable of being the kind of people and doing the kind of things that most Middle Americans applaud. Yet U-Hab and the poor are proving almost everyone wrong.

The Renegades of Harlem, whose twenty Black and Puerto Rican members range in age from eighteen to thirty-five, converted their first six-story, 23-unit tenement for an average cost of $15,000 per unit in just one year's time. Universally poor and uneducated, almost all with criminal records, the gang members were able to not only personally rehabilitate the building, but they also managed the dispersement of funds from the mortgage loan for materials and supplies. The gang went by the book, learning all the traditional business rules as they went along, even forming a corporation with seven of their members on the board. The homesteader/workers earned a training stipend of $3.00 per hour while working on the building so that they, hopefully, can develop careers and steady incomes in the building trades.

In addition, each worker volunteers thousands of hours of Sweat Equity "free time" to assure that the best workers will be able to live in the most desirable completed apartments. The corporation will own the building, which will be operated as a co-operative by the people who worked so hard to make it happen. Monthly charges (rent) are projected at $152 for a one-bedroom apartment, which is substantially less than the usual New York market rate for a decent living environment.

The hardest workers—the ones who put in the most free-time sweat equity—get the choicest apartments. This competition soon turns the Renegades into top-flight rehabbers.

The Renegades are also restoring a seven-unit building at an average unit cost of $16,000; a four-unit building at an average cost of $17,000; and a second seven-unit building at an average cost of $16,000. Over one hundred people are now involved in learning the construction trades as they earn their own homes through these Renegade-controlled projects. Hundreds more are waiting to taste the joy of working, learning, and being an "owner" of property which one can be proud of on a street one can call home.

There's no better feeling than turning an impossiblity into something possible.

Philip St. Georges is director of U-Hab, a

Cum Laude graduate of Yale University, and also the owner of a one-bedroom co-op apartment in the first Sweat Equity project of them all. On Columbus Avenue next to a tire store, this modest brick building represents thousands of hours of effort by six prospective homeowners who saved it from the wrecker's ball. They call it La Casa de Sol, partly because an exterior wall had fallen off the back of the building so that the sun shone in, and partly because their contribution to the saving of the building has brought new psychic sunshine into their own lives.

It took more than two years to complete the renovation of the building. Thirty-two garbage bins of accumulated trash had to be hauled from inside the building because former neighbors used the windowless building as a public garbage dump. The central beam supporting the building had fallen down, the fifth-floor outside wall had fallen off, all the floors were broken, yet the six homesteaders were able to do basic rehabilitation for $4,500 per unit and completed the job for a total of $7,000 per unit.

Three of the rehabbers were young women, all except St. Georges were unemployed and very poor. Yet, today, all residents of the La Casa de Sol have found employment, are property owners, are contributing members of the community.

Their efforts have inspired four more buildings on the block to be rehabilitated.

Bring the abandoned people and the abandoned buildings together.

St. Georges was an idealist when he first became involved with the poor people who wished to take the initiative in rehabilitating their housing and the community in which they lived, themselves. Now he has become a pragmatic believer in urban homesteading for the poor. The federal and local governments continue to spend billions of dollars each year on the traditional welfare system. He sees these billions better spent in bringing the 150,000 abandoned dwelling units together with the over 500,000 unemployed people in New York City. It could be the quickest, most sensible employment, training, housing, motivating, neighborhood-saving program imaginable.

It costs New York City $3,000 to seal up an abandoned building and $6,000 to demolish it. Then the Federal department of Housing and Urban Development cost guidelines permit newly constructed or substantially rehabilitated housing to have total development costs of approximately

St. Georges' own co-op apartment shows the results of the city's first sweat-equity project. Sunlight and green plants brighten what was once a building ready for demolition.

$45,000 per unit. Section 8 Housing Assistance Payment subsidies can provide very low income families with rental assistance payments up to $700 per month to occupy this housing.

By contrast, urban homesteading through U-Hab can totally rehabilitate a structure at a cost of $21,000 or less per unit, which translates to total monthly rental expenses of approximately $200. This also includes the added benefits of the new homesteader learning a trade, giving him self-confidence, and allowing him to become a homeowner or renter with a sense of responsibility for his home and his neighborhood. The "sweat equity" part of the U-Hab equation not only cuts reconstruction costs in half, it doubles the benefits to the rehabber.

New York City, the greatest of all cities with the greatest of all urban problems, also has the greatest potential for finding solutions to those problems. The brownstoners, although still struggling, are coming back to the city and liking it. The artists and young families, by transforming deserted industrial lofts into homes throughout the SoHo and Tribeca districts of Manhattan, have created a new national life-style. The pre-dominantly Black community of Bedford-Stuyvesant has used the more traditional forms of revitalization procedures to re-create a middle-class neighborhood of handsome homes and strong identity.

But there remains the poor, the very poor. And now comes an even greater test for a city with miles of buildings which often have few of the aesthetically redeeming virtues of stained glass and hand-carved wood. These are working-class buildings which house a people who have no work. Can a universally condemned welfare system be transformed into a self-help system? Can a revolution in thinking about old buildings, in attitudes about people, in the economics of urban living, take place which can allow the poor to participate in the rebuilding of their own future?

What was once a middle-class movement of historic preservation can now be expanded to embrace the more basic concept of urban conservation. This could be the American solution to more than the revitalization of its cities—the revitalization of its people. This crazy idea is beginning to work in New York City, and if it can succeed there, it can succeed anywhere.

The Nicest City to Come Back to:
Savannah

In this new age of urban preservation, Savannah is one of the nation's first "model cities." It has been able to wisely and sensitively save and restore the cream of its priceless old architecture, and now it is just as sensitively attempting to deal with the proverbial burr under the blanket of urban preservation—assuring a mixture of urban residents which include the wealthy, the middle income, and the poor.

Savannah is a city twice-blessed. Even its arch-enemy, Yankee General William T. Sherman, could not countenance the destruction of this exquisitely designed Georgia coastal city when he swept the South in 1864. The city that was the dream of James Oglethorpe in 1733 was spared, and Sherman dispatched his famous telegram to President Lincoln: "I beg to present you, as a Christmas gift, the City of Savannah."

And today its friends, the people who have been working for over twenty years to assure that it will continue to be one of the most livable cities in America, have presented Savannah to us all.

Oglethorpe's planning concept of creating the city around a series of public squares or parks beginning at the Savannah River continues today. Each square is the nucleus of each ward or neighborhood, which helps create a strong community identity and links each neighborhood with the others. As new wards and squares were built, each was developed to respect the character and scale of the older squares. Today the city of Savannah is a brilliant tapestry of oak-lined streets and exquisite eighteenth- and nineteenth-century architecture, linked by an emerald chain of carefully tended squares which are filled with sculpture, comfortable benches, and people. Savannah fits one like an old velvet slipper. It is reasonable to the mind, logically moving from square to square.

Probably because of the city's superb logic and reasonableness, its people move with an assurance, grace, and quiet good will which is foreign to most harried city residents. Even the auto must slow down for Oglethorpe's squares, driving carefully around them instead of through them. Yet there seems to be no traffic "problem." The people walk more because there is so much to see, and each square seems to hold a friend who is willing to pass the time of day instead of kill it.

The squares are Savannah's living rooms, their walls the vegetation, street furniture, and buildings around them. And probably because Savannahians tend to truly live in their city instead of becoming encapsulated in high-rise apartments and suburban-bound automobiles, they saw the signs of impending destruction of their city sooner and reacted to it more decisively.

Savannah's luxuriant twenty squares are surrounded by architecture one would expect to find sheltered under glass in a museum. But here history and beauty still live amid the vibrant bustle of the city, housing real people and a sure sense of the future.

The first twenty years of our existence, we were in a crisis situation.

Savannah had survived epidemics, the great fires of 1796 and 1820, and the Revolutionary and Civil wars, but in the 1950s the greatest threat of all came in the name of progress. The city had suffered an economic decline after the First World War as well as suffering the FHA-inspired migration to the suburbs after the Second World War. By the 1950s, the only solution for city revival seemed to be more parking lots.

But the intended destruction of the fine Georgian-style Davenport House for a funeral home parking lot proved to be the flash point for Savannah's preservationists. Led by Mrs. Anna Hunter, nine ladies formed the Historic Savannah

Foundation. They soon saved the house and then went on to complete a survey of 2,500 homes in the 2.2-mile center city, finding some 1,100 to be historically or architecturally important.

Under the leadership of Leopold Adler II, Historic Savannah created one of the first preservation revolving loan funds with the help of local businessmen and bankers. The money has been used to purchase properties which are deteriorating and then to resell them, with design restrictions, to people who are willing to restore and maintain them.

As interest in the community became re-energized, people who had left for the suburbs or for other parts of the nation began to return. Miles B. Lane, who headed Georgia's largest bank in Atlanta, came back to Savannah to begin his own private renewal of the city. He bought

Business and pleasure mix beautifully, thanks to Savannah's parklike downtown. A 1904 auto garage converted to offices and shops on one corner, the oldest operating U.S. theater on the other, and breathtakingly beautiful nineteenth-century homes all around.

and restored several old houses, selling them to other returning citizens. He also restored entire blocks of homes occupied by the poor, then rented them back to the same occupants at the same rent they paid before renovation.

Sparked by the efforts of Historic Savannah and by individuals such as Lane, today practically every one of the original 1,100 surveyed houses has been restored. The battle to save the historic heart of Savannah has been won, but the war goes on. Audrey Rhangos, present acting director of the Historic Savannah Foundation, sees the organization now moving into a new area of positive programs to influence rehabilitation of housing, to influence the more sociological aspect of the back-to-the-city movement, and to help in guiding compatible new in-fill construction.

The Foundation's concerns are now directed to the Victorian District, a forty-block area of post-1850s homes just south of the older Historic Landmark District. Another study has shown that there are over three hundred structures which are of architectural importance there in need of protection. In addition, the revolving fund is now being used to purchase Façade Easements from homeowners of restored historic homes in order to protect their exteriors from misguided improvements. By using a relatively small amount of money as leverage to make bigger things happen, Historic Savannah has sparked millions of dollars of restoration work by private individuals and by other organizations.

We buy out slum landlords, then restore the houses for the tenants.

One of the most exciting preservation spinoffs of Historic Savannah's efforts has been the Savannah Landmark Rehabilitation Project, or SNAP. Formed by Leopold Adler II and a twenty-three-member board of white and Black community leaders, it is attempting to meet both the problems of deterioration and displacement head on. SNAP is now in the process of buying out the slumlords who have been allowing the homes to deteriorate, taking the first steps in purchasing and restoring the first of 600 of the 1,200 structures in the Victorian District. Then with the help of federal subsidy programs, the

Preservation for all the people. The Savannah Landmark Rehabilitation Project (SNAP) makes it happen. Slums turned into historic homes by the people who live there.

organization will rent the homes back to the poor tenants at rents they can afford.

Beth Lattimore Reiter, director of SNAP, projects that thirty or more buildings will be restored each year. Costs will be held to under $12,000 per unit by hiring local unemployed people under a federal CETA grant to learn the building trades as they work under professional supervision. The back-to-the-city movement by the middle income and a viable stay-in-the-city effort by the poor can be compatible, she says. The SNAP concept not only saves the houses but it also saves intact the original community of people. Costs are much less, both socially and monetarily, than building traditional public-housing projects.

Savannah has always enjoyed racial and economic diversity, with each city block expressing a checkerboard of races and incomes. The unique working relationship of Historic Savannah restoring buildings for the people coming back to the city, and SNAP restoring homes for the people already living in the city, has created an encouraging promise for a continuing, pluralistic society.

Here we try to work with the housing stock we have.

Frank Butler is the director of the Savannah Housing and Redevelopment Authority. While some HRA officials in other cities are downright antagonistic to preservationists, seeing them as somehow in competition with urban renewal, Mr. Butler expresses the uniqueness of the Savannah experience. His agency's philosophy is re-use, smaller and more manageable development proj-

Another example of SNAP's version of "low-income housing." Beautiful architecture rescued from slumlords, restored, and rented again to the same tenants at a price they can afford.

ects, and public-money enhancement of private preservation efforts.

One of the city's most dramatic examples of their enlightened philosophy is Savannah's magnificent revitalized, multi-use waterfront. The historic Factor's Row of four- and five-story commercial buildings once housed the city's great cotton industry. Now it houses dozens of busy restaurants, pubs, shops, and museums on the lower wharf side. Some of the second and third floors of the ancient brick and stone buildings are being converted into apartments and more shops. And the top floors, which face the opposite Bay Street side, house business offices, including the Savannah Chamber of Commerce. But it was the Savannah HRA's investment of $7 million which transformed the riverside into a spectacular pedestrian park that paved the way for the dra-

matic and creative private investments which have occurred.

The public has made its wishes known. It wants only the kind of progress that preservation can bring. City officials, from the mayor on down, understand the economic dynamics of preservation and respect the public's concern. There are few cities where public and private interests have worked so well together for the general public good. And it pays. In prerestoration 1963, tourism contributed $6 million to Savannah's economy. In 1973, tourism contributed $47 million. Presently, a $100 million annual rate is not impossible.

Nobody has regretted moving downtown.

Savannah's waterfront is one of the finest historic commercial transformations in the nation. A handsome example of co-operation between public agencies and private investors to create a dynamic multi-use complex.

Audrey Rhangos was born in Savannah, and like so many of her generation, her parents moved to the suburbs when she was still a child. But also like so many of her generation, she has come back. She said it seemed to occur to all of her friends all at once, around 1970, that interesting things were happening back downtown. They got involved with the Historic Savannah Foundation, then finally made the ultimate commitment by purchasing old houses and restoring them. Nobody has regretted it, she said, and nobody that she knows would live anywhere else. It's been a wonderful life, they've lived in beautiful houses that few would have been able to afford anywhere else, and they have taken part in something that is critical to the revitalization of the whole city. That's a lot to get for your money.

It must have been especially worth it to Ms. Rhangos, even in those early days when she was still a little afraid to walk on the streets and when she anxiously watched her children play outside. Hers is one of the many big nineteenth-century homes, a Queen Anne-style house with one of the city's biggest live oaks shading an over-sized side yard. A gracious home able to make

Audrey Rhangos said it seemed to occur to all of her friends at once to return to the city. With the ultimate commitment of owning your own home in the city, you are part of a life-style that stretches back for generations.

It's a wonderful life, says Ms. Rhangos, to live in beautiful houses that few would have been able to afford anywhere else. The carved marble mantles, the rare wood detailing, it could all last forever if people care.

children and friends feel comfortable, yet it manages still to display period furniture and furnishings of museum quality. From its carved-marble fireplaces to its etched-glass doors, the house quietly assures the visitor that it indeed is historic, it is restored, and it intends to provide the most gracious hospitality for many years to come.

It's like a three-decker mobile home.

The charm of Savannah is its diversity, and its homes are no exception. Sam Adams and his wife, Berta, own a townhouse on West Jones Street that is much smaller than Audrey's but no less delightful. Only fourteen feet wide and fifty-five feet long, this 1886 Italianate is one of a pair, both bought by Sam in 1973.

He was living out of town at the time, and only went on a neighborhood house tour because his mother wanted company. By the time the tour was over, he discovered that he had been the last visitor out of every house, and he knew that he had to have one for his own. He moved back to Savannah, rented an apartment in the neighborhood, and began his search.

This building was the one he liked and the one he could afford. And it was wide open. A flophouse for transient winos, the little townhouse also housed over one thousand wine bottles as well as assorted trash. He and an old carpenter slowly transformed the neglected flophouse into an airy, multilevel home.

Today the stairwell forms a bright three-story atrium. The spacious rooms are sun-filled and modern, transforming the old structure into a youthful and comfortable living environment. It's

Berta and Sam Adams live in a modern home that is over ninety years old. Tranformed from a depository of derelicts' trash, it is now bright, efficient, and supremely comfortable.

the most convenient and utilitarian house he's ever been in, Sam says. And Berta says she likes the close, urban feel of the neighborhood. So many other young couples are fixing up the houses around them. There is a community co-operative grocery store right on the corner, filled with fresh apples and pumpkins and things you can't find in big stores.

The oak trees nod their branches against the windows and folks say hi as they walk by, on their way to the store or on to the next square. You know your neighbors and they know you. Where could there be a nicer place to live than this? she asks.

Within two or three blocks, we have a dozen friends.

Somewhere between the Queen Anne mansion and the Adamses' exquisite minature townhouse lie the many larger townhouses similar to the one on East Charlton owned by Tommy and Elaine Austin. Its elegant exterior of brick and wrought iron reveal an interior that combines the best of the old with a comfortable, modern sense of design and space.

When they purchased the badly deteriorated building in 1971, the Austins gutted the interior, opening the rear of the house to the sylvan quiet of a secluded backyard. While the front rooms still maintain much of the formal elegance of their past, the back rooms seem almost suburban as they look out through the large multipaned windows to the shrubs and ferns below. This family has brought uptown and out-of-town together, preserving the historic character of the street while expressing the uniqueness of their own life inside.

The Adamses' fourteen-foot-wide Italianate town-house is one of a pair that were so badly deteriorated no one else would buy them.

Tom and Elaine Austin with daughter, Harriet, in the more traditional front part of their home.

The rear section of the Austins' home reflects Tom's appreciation of more contemporary southern comfort.

The back courtyard brings the country into the city, giving the Austins the best of both urban and suburban worlds.

The Austin townhouse, where everything is within walking distance, including a dozen friends.

But life was never like this in the suburbs, says Tommy Austin. Everything's within walking distance, with the meat market just across the square, the drugstore in the back of the block, the grocery store just four blocks away. There are concerts in the square for the old folks who live in a nursing home just a block away, and sometimes the neighbors just bring their card tables and drinks and a hot dish to the square on a nice summer evening. All their friends are living around them now it seems, and the ones still out in the suburbs, well, they come visiting a lot more lately.

Maybe the story of Savannah has something to do with estrangement, or the lack of it. Residences and businesses never were separated. There never really were large ghettos created by color or income because everyone had always lived together in the general areas and often on the same streets. Even the houses built on speculation or for rental use tried to respect the streetscape and the sense of architectural style.

Commercial buildings today are either old ones beautifully refinished or new ones that are sensitive to the style and scale of their residential neighbors. The streets, the squares, are all part of one's home and living space. The squares provide stability to the city, resisting the rush to automobilize the nation. They force the driver encapsulated in his automobile to slow down, the philosopher trees and green grass invite him to stop and walk and talk. So the pace of life is a little slower here. And as anybody on any Savannah street corner will tell you, life is a whole lot better here, too, for the people who have recently returned to the city and for the ones who have never left.

Next to the Adamses and just down the street from the Austins and Audrey Rhangos, and the rest of Savannah, is the Food Co-Op. What was counterculture has become a part of everybody's life in this truly diverse urban environment.

Getting a New Lease on Life: Galveston

Few American cities have experienced the ups and downs of fortune, the disasters and defeats, as has this sun-baked, seductive old port city which lies on the coast of Texas in the Gulf of Mexico. From the 1840s to 1900, it was known as the "Queen City of the Southwest." When cotton was king in the South's economy, Galveston was the shipping, banking, and cultural queen of the Southland west of the Mississippi.

Although some scoffed at the city as nothing but an overgrown sandbar, the enriched merchants and shipowners covered the sand with a blanket of the finest Greek, Roman, Romanesque, Renaissance Revival, Italianate, Victorian, and Moderne architecture anywhere. Whether small raised cottages, luxurious private palaces, or cast-iron-front commercial buildings, each expressed an exuberance of style that gave it a unique Galvestonian personality.

But in 1900, a hurricane blew out of the Gulf to turn this bustling, queenly city into a devastated mile-and-a-half long sandbar. More than six thousand people were drowned and thousands of the beautiful buildings were either washed away or badly damaged. Instead of fleeing, the citizens stayed. They immediately began the mammoth task of raising the entire island by six or more feet, raising all the buildings and then pouring sea-dredged sand underneath. Then they built a sea wall around the island.

In 1915, another hurricane came, some say it was even worse than the first, but the city survived. Yet, finally, economic winds accomplished what nature's winds could not. The growth of Houston fifty miles to the north, the building of the Houston Ship Channel, and the growth of inland railroads caused many people to leave for greener economic pastures. Even gambling, which caused a short economic upturn in the 1950s, and the sun, which brought visitors to come sit on the warm summer sand, could not stem the exodus or the deterioration of the often abandoned old buildings.

Yet Galveston's pride died hard. In 1971, a referendum to allow a major urban renewal project to demolish many of the nineteenth-century residential and commercial buildings was defeated five to one.

We are picking up the pieces of the puzzle of what was a perfect and beautiful city.

This brush with another disaster shocked the citizens and especially the Junior League of Galveston. They wisely attacked the problem at its source, the Strand which was once called the "Wall Street of the Southwest." This seedy street of run-down brick commercial buildings was the symbol of the economic decay of the city. In the

The Strand, "Wall Street of the Southwest," in the 1870s, has become one of the most exciting streets of commercial re-use projects in the 1970s. An almost perfect streetscape of cast-iron-front buildings stretch as far as the eye can see.

early 1970s, thanks to new paint and new interest, this street began the transformation into what Philadelphia planner Edmund Bacon has declared "the finest concentration of nineteenth-century commercial structures I have ever seen."

The League purchased and restored two buildings, encouraging the Galveston County Cultural Arts Council to locate their offices in one of them. The Arts Council, in turn, hired Emily Whiteside, former associate director of the Texas Arts Commission in Austin, to investigate how the city could increase its cultural vitality. She came for a few months and was captivated by the architecture. She soon formed a realization that while culture followed the growing economic richness of Galveston in the 1800s, today the architectural culture expressed in its structures and in the desires of its community could again generate

economic strength. The richness, the value, of a unique city was already there. Now was only the job of putting the pieces together again, to re-create the beautiful and perfect seaport city.

Whiteside stayed on as executive director of the Arts Council, an organization of eighty arts and cultural groups. To broaden the scope of preservation activity, the Galveston Historical Foundation, in 1973, established a revolving fund to protect and hold for new uses buildings along the Strand. Thanks to the efforts of these groups, the Strand was designated a National Historic Landmark District and nineteen buildings are now being restored for an exciting mixture of retail, office, and residential uses.

Residential use of commercial warehouses is not new, with pioneer efforts occurring in New York City's SoHo district and in other eastern

Private investors, with guidance from the Galveston Historical Foundation, are restoring the sturdy commercial buildings into a dynamic mix of fine restaurants, shops, offices, and apartments.

reclaimed waterfront neighborhood, with flop hotels, garbage, and vagrants littering the streets, proved an interesting living environment for an attractive, slightly built single woman. The almost abandoned commercial area was often so deserted that she could walk her dog in the alley while wearing her bathrobe.

The restoration of the building, which was a former printing shop and warehouse, became a personal battle. She cleaned much of the generations of grime and refuse out of its three floors herself. She managed to live in the structure while workmen hammered and sawed around her. Once, a late night storm flooded her living room, so she spent the early morning hours attempting to move

Emily Whiteside began the revitalization of the Strand when she purchased an 1870 former printing plant and transformed it into three spacious flats, one on each floor, with a ground-floor rental space for a shop.

cities, but the Strand adds some extra amenities to this intriguing way of living. Galveston is one of the few cities where some of the alleys behind the three- and four-story commercial buildings, which Whiteside calls "storm-shuttered thruways," have been placed on the National Register. Many of the second- and third-story apartments in the restored buildings have front and rear entrances, so the resident can use the entire environment around his red-bricked and comfortable home.

The first person to take the plunge in this ultimate in urban living was Emily Whiteside. She purchased a three-story, cast-iron-front building which is 20 feet wide and 152 feet long. The dimensions in themselves posed interesting interior design considerations. And the still-un-

A new atrium stairwell was opened through the middle of the Whiteside Flats to bring light to the interior rooms. The small courtyard is a dramatic entrance for every apartment.

heavy antique furniture out of the way of the cascade of water pouring through a leaky skylight.

But it is easy for her to laugh at the horror stories of the past as she now enjoys the present. Her home of twelve-foot ceilings, double-hung eleven-foot-high windows, old brick walls and the mellow yellow of heart pine floors are the catalyst which is now causing a building boom of residences on the upper floors of the Strand.

I just wouldn't want to live anywhere else in Galveston.

One of her tenants in the 1870 building's two additional apartment units is Peter Brink, execu-

Ms. Whiteside's own home in the three-story industrial building features a 20 x 25-foot living room with a skylighted roof and a backyard garden.

tive director of the Galveston Historical Foundation. A former lawyer and preservationist from Washington, D.C., he came to set up the Foundation's revolving fund. Like Emily and so many others, he was captivated by the architecture and the cosmopolitan attitude of the people, and he stayed.

Peter and his landlord exemplify the kind of people who are attracted to urban living on the Strand: imaginative, dynamic, and often single. It is exciting living among the many good restaurants and shops which are blooming like magnolia blossoms behind the iron and brick façades of the buildings. There is always the changing street scene of strangers and "locals," the sheer impact of other people on one's consciousness, which urbanologist Jane Jacobs calls "the ballet of the streets." The Arts Council and the Foundation are encouraging this "ballet" with two annual events, Dickens's Evening on the Strand and the Festival on the Strand, which draw over thirty thousand people to each event.

Another Strand residential amenity is the living spaces themselves which are attracting a growing number of private owners who are restoring the buildings on an individual basis. Creative preservationists can take the approximately four thousand square feet per floor of a Strand industrial building and transform that space into a mixture of shops, offices, and apartments which aesthetically work, allowing the stores to draw the daily street ballet for the apartment or condominium dwellers to look down upon.

But the question which many cynical bankers, insurance companies, and politicians ask is, "What about economic feasibility?" Young developers like Robert Lynch, who is also the grandson of an original builder of the Strand, can answer, "Yes, preservation does pay, better than you think."

By purchasing a deteriorated three-story building for as little as $35,000 and investing a couple of hundred thousand dollars in rehabilitation, some of which can be paid in sweat equity, a person can create a commercial-residential complex that is aesthetically pleasing, economical for the tenants, and a sound investment. Many people forget that the "value" of a building or a piece of property is only worth what a person will pay for

Peter Brink, like a growing number of people, wouldn't think of living anywhere else but on the Strand. This is where the action is, including several fine restaurants which make dramatic use of the enormous industrial building space.

it. The simple psychological twist of a public's attitude about an area can make the difference. If it is considerad a slum, a "bad" place, a sturdy building can be worth a few thousand dollars or nothing. If the area is considered an exciting place, a place of historic and cultural value, that same building can be worth hundreds of thousands of dollars.

Lynch still chuckles at the memory of attempting to convince his father of this fact. It took two days and nights of argument and figuring to prove to his father, a new-construction developer from California, that a deteriorated old building could actually be more profitable than a new-from-the-ground-up development. And the investment is especially appealing when, like so many people on the Strand, the developer calls his building "home" as well as an investment.

With four-story buildings still selling for as little as $75,000 on the Strand as late as 1977, there is little surprise that enterprising buyers and renters are coming from as far away as Dallas and New York to taste the excitement of what was only a couple of years ago just a street for a few wholesale food merchants and derelicts.

Purchasing an old home takes a whole new dimension of personal commitment.

Robert Lynch, grandson of one of the founders of the Strand, has restored one of the three-story brick buildings for use as shops and apartments.

Lynch's own apartment shows an imaginative use of the large loft space. A kitchen/bathroom module was built in the center of the space, with a sleeping loft above. The living-room area looks out onto the street activity of the Strand below.

Just a few blocks away, an easy walk from the Strand, there are two Historical Districts of homes in Galveston. Called the East End Historical District and the Silk Stocking Historical Precinct, they contain over eight hundred architecturally important structures. The pleasing spectrum of Victorian frame houses to grand mansions dramatically expresses the history of the city. And equally important, they still are the homes of a diverse group of residents which cover the spectrum of age, race, and income.

But like the rest of the city, the disasters of the past have taken their toll. Some buildings are abandoned, others are neglected and underutilized. Recently, an interesting combination of new residents have arrived to restore many of the buildings which were so sadly deteriorated in the past. Some of the newcomers are older,

wealthy couples who have seen the revitalization efforts on the Strand and now think it is safe to invest in a vacation home in the surrounding residential areas. But most of the new residents are people who see the palm-lined streets as home, a place to spend the rest of their lives.

Although young couples with children are drawn to the nineteenth-century homes with the big backyards, an interesting social change is expressed in the single people who are perfectly willing to take on the responsibility of a big "family" home.

Dr. Robinson purchased an 1856 Louisiana-style cottage about four years ago, and has worked hard to transform it into a fine melding of gracious living with modern conveniences. But the doctor is not the typical homeowner, because first the doctor is young and single, and

Only a few blocks separate the activity of the Strand from the East End Historical District. Dr. Sally Robinson has restored this 1856 Louisiana-style cottage and also organized the local neighborhood association.

Dr. Robinson's house exemplifies the unique Galveston architecture with its many porches and large windows which let the cool evening air circulate through every room.

second the doctor is a woman. Dr. Sally Robinson is a pediatrician who came to the University of Texas Medical Branch in Galveston to study, and then decided to stay. She purchased the raised, one-and-one-half-story house because she liked it. Built by a ship's carpenter, the house is snugly crafted of wood, with tall windows and doors that open to catch every breeze.

Sally Robinson also helped organize the East End Historical District Association and is now its president. They are concerned with neighborhood traffic and parking, code enforcement, and also with the need for garbage-can racks in the alleys.

In her four years of working on her house and with the neighborhood, she has learned to appreciate the extra dimension of personal commitment which an old house demands. It is not just a superficial kick, this preservation business. You not only invest your money. You also invest a part of yourself.

She is also aware that more single people are taking on old-house restoration. She interprets it as symbolic in the development of a new American life-style where a single person can do his or her own thing without being thought of as a weird or eccentric person. She also feels that a single person can better give the amount of emotional energy which restoration of a structure with all its attendant problems requires.

A single person does not have all the diverse demands which a married couple has, both from the demands of the spouse and of the children. The single person can become more single-minded, able to give the old house more time and effort. The old house becomes both the process and the goal, an activity which may turn not only a profit in dollars but in personal growth and satisfaction as well.

To many young people, the back-to-the-city movement has become a form of a new utopia, a new direction to be taken after the dead-ends of Vietnam, the Age of Aquarius, and the suburbs. People who have imagination and ideals, who are willing to go beyond what the average person asks of himself in order to accomplish something, often end up on the front porch of an old house scraping paint. Creating the future out of a discarded past can often be the greatest high there is. And if one has the dreams and the energy of youth, the high can often be carried into old age.

I don't want to live in a museum. I want something I can be comfortable in.

In new houses, too, doorknobs fall off and rats and roaches crawl in. But the practicality of most Galvestonian preservationists demands that their old houses be as shipshape and watertight as the barks and brigantines which used to sail out of the harbor. Bob Clark has been working on his house

Bob Clark's ancestors would have felt very much at home in his 1894 Queen Anne. His patient, personal restoration of this extraordinary house has made it a source of pride for the entire neighborhood.

for three years now. He wanted to do it right. Until he bought a flower business a short while ago, it had been his sole occupation and obsession.

He drove down from Dallas one day and went house hunting. When the salesman stopped at this battered 1894 Queen Anne, three-story house, Bob didn't want to go in because it looked so bad. But once he stepped inside and saw the handcrafted pine and oak woodwork and the sunburst designs above the windows, he bought it on the spot. He paid $36,000 for it and his friends said he paid too much. Now as he walks through the 8,000-square-foot house and points to the matching carriage house and the studio apartment in back, he ventures that his friends might have been wrong.

Clark is also young and single, with a great deal of energy. For the first year, he commuted six hundred miles each weekend from Dallas to work on his house. He came to Galveston for the house. He only began looking for a job after he was reasonably sure about the love affair with his home.

He enjoys it when people step into the foyer and their eyes get big, shocked by the spectacular craftsmanship of the woodwork. That is what sold him on the house in the first place, and he is continually delighted by a carpenter who almost a hundred years ago had carefully laid three-inch strips of Georgia pine in such marvelous geometric patterns on the walls, the ceilings, everywhere.

Clark appreciates the crazy purity of that carpenter, and he reflects it as he refinishes the floors, stripping them on hands and knees, figuring that it took a lot of years for past residents to put those marks on the wide pine boards, so why take them off and have a new floor you could find in a split-level?

> *You've got to start somewhere. You need to invest yourself in something.*

There are many Victorian cottages at the edge of the East End Historical District. Some have been rental units for years and have slowly deteriorated. A few years ago, you could have bought any along the block for under $10,000. But few people did until the Historic District was formed and people began to get the idea that old was respectable again.

Mike Doherty, a young and single bank employee, wanted to make his mark on the community. He was born on the island, he had a good job now, and a little 1881 double-dormered cottage was something he thought he could invest in. He also invested his energy, spending hours and hours in scraping, stripping, and repairing the sturdy house.

Then he married his wife, Weez, about halfway through the restoration process, so they both were able to finish the long effort which transforms a shabby house into a comfortable home. He was the first new owner-resident on the block for many years. Now several other young couples are restoring the houses around them.

Every room in Bob Clark's house holds another surprise of multitudes of varnished wood set in geometric patterns. This is no house for modern decoration, and Clark enjoys re-creating its authentic Victorian atmosphere.

Mike and Weez Doherty sit under the double dormers of their 1881 cottage. They have scraped, sanded, and painted to create every young couple's dream house.

One of the last projects in their program of restoration has been the nursery. Weez and Mike completed the job just in time as they wait behind the white picket fence for the newest Galvestonian on the block to make its appearance.

A city of 64,000 people Galveston is proving that "urban preservation" is not restricted to big cities. Wherever there is a diversity of old architecture and of people, wherever there is a neighborhood which is ignored, abandoned, or underutilized, there is a place for a renewed sense of community.

The old houses are the catalyst. People who can see past the peeled paint and broken windows are the process. The result can be a newer, happier outlook on life for the whole community, with people seated on their front porches or looking out their apartment windows, waiting for the next generation to come by.

Breakfast areas need not be stuffy in an old house, and the Doherty's have proved it. A sun porch, arbor, and dining room combined, it shows that old houses can be more fun than anything else.

PART THREE

The Struggle to Preserve

On July 15, 1972, a lady from Brooklyn sent a letter to the city of Portland, Oregon. "Dear Sir," she wrote, "So you are tearing down the First National Bank of Oregon's 1916 building in Portland. I've never been to Portland. It is not my concern. But it is my concern!!! Come look at the wonderful progress we have made in New York City. The buildings use all available ground space. They make money for the builder. But also, take a look at the dead faces of the people who work in those buildings.

"God! Please stop destroying the beauty of our country. If our eyes see no beauty . . . then our behavior has no beauty . . . and we become criminals.

"Please, somebody do something. Save at least this building."

Over half of all the buildings ever listed on the National Register of Historic Sites have now been demolished. Since 1949, urban renewal has come to twelve hundred cities in America with fistsful of dollars to tear down some of the finest neighborhoods we have ever had or will ever have again. Freeways have laid waste entire cities, eviscerating the last bit of vitality and unique identity from them in order to "save" them. Residents stand helplessly by as a corporate property owner demolishes a key city landmark for yet another parking lot.

People cry out in the hysteria of loss as everything they know, everything they remember, slowly crumbles away. They are left in a strange new landscape of blacktopped memories and a plasticized, franchised future. "Please, somebody do something," they cry, wondering how it all happened, and why.

Who do we blame for this trashing of America? Who do we put on trial for the dehumanizing of our cities? As was said in a Pogo comic strip several years ago, "I have seen the enemy and it is us." America's great virtues of optimism and self-confidence are also our greatest vices. We are the world's *nouveau riche,* the brash young country with more money than sense, the "ugly Americans" of insensitivity and unlimited power.

In less than three hundred years, we have plundered, paved, plastered an entire continent. Our genius for technology has accelerated the advancement of commercial growth a hundredfold, moving us from a nation of oxcarts, to river commerce, to railroads, to autos, to jet planes. We have leaped from Colonial architecture to Federal, to Victorian, to Sullivan, to Le Corbusier, to McDonald's. And most destructive of all, we have grown from a nation of a few hundred thousand to over 300 million people, each wishing to leave his bold imprint on the fabric of our society.

We quickly moved from a nation of farmers to a nation of great cities, the focus of our unbridled creative talent and developmental urges. We celebrated the cities with statues and marvelous public buildings to contain our pride. But then the Great Depression came like an economic plague, causing us to lose confidence in the city as our economic and social heartbeat. The Second World War came along just in time to help us regain our confidence in ourselves but never again for our cities. Prosperity after the war gave many of us the option of leaving the old memories and old buildings. Governmental decisions assured and subsidized our flight.

A recent study by the Rand Corporation and the National League of Cities helps define the dynamics behind America's flight to the suburbs. First, what began as a wartime effort became a peacetime obsession—the building of the interstate freeway system. The freeways not only encouraged the U.S. automobile industry to greater production and greater control over the national economy, it also opened up great areas of suburban land for more intensive development.

Then the federal government followed with the Federal Housing Act and government-backed mortgages to make it easy for people to leave the city and build new homes near those efficient new freeways. Thanks to additional federal water and sewer grants for swift proliferation of suburban housing tracts, the people who could left the cities to the people who could not, the poor.

Finally, to add insult to injury, the federal government allowed mortgage interest payments and property taxes to be deducted from federal income taxes, providing a massive subsidy which went primarily to the affluent who now lived away from the cities. And the federal government sealed the city's doom by creating urban-renewal programs to tear down the still-sturdy middle-income housing of central cities, replacing it with high-rise "low income" housing which repelled even the poorest of the poor.

If the federal government, and we as its constituency, would have planned to systematically destroy the cities and everything of value in them, we could not have done a better job.

Seldom in urban developments does the new allow the old to remain. An exception is in Boston, where the 102-year-old Trinity Church still reflects on the glass skin of the sixty-story John Hancock Tower.

The End of Optimism and the Beginning of Hope

There is a little Babbitt in us all: the acceptance of the easy answer, the dream of riches at the expense of others. But, fortunately, we as a nation seem to be learning and maturing. The downtown chambers of commerce are learning that the freeway is not an avenue for new suburbanite customers to drive into their city stores, but an escape hatch for even more of their old customers to leave. Tearing down the old downtown buildings for a new suburban-type shopping mall destroys what uniqueness their city had and now makes them just another cookie-cutter suburban mall competing with all the others.

Even the city planner and the architect are learning. Although the 1930s concept of the wide avenues and broad green spaces and gigantic buildings of the City Beautiful looked good on paper, they were dehumanizing and devitalizing when built. The Bauhaus school of architecture with its right angles and minimal emotion won design awards but lost the sense of humanity as well as the sense of the city. It was only later when the experts learned that people were what really mattered, with their need for human-scale physical relationships and close spatial continuity. Even more important, people seemed to need a spiritual continuity, too, a continuing relationship with old buildings, spaces, events. The monuments, the historic buildings, had more intrinsic value than as perches for pigeons.

Today, we seem to have awakened from our drunken, decades-long orgy of exploitation of our

Preservation is an educational process. Too often, we must personally witness the ravaging of our heritage and our neighborhoods before we are moved to become involved. But then, a healthy sense of controlled rage can cause us to accomplish things of which we didn't think we were capable. (Photo courtesy Old Town Restorations, Inc. and James Wengler.)

natural and built resources. A growing number of modern urban pioneers is venturing back to the city, grasping at the still-standing architectural treasures as if searching for jewels in a dustbin. And the people who are already there, knee-deep in abandoned buildings, are doing their own treasure hunting among the sorry streets that even their landlords discarded as slums.

The reality of a national return to the city has also filtered up to the federal government. In 1977, Congress appropriated $17.5 million under the National Historic Preservation Act for community preservation programs. Although this is a tremendous increase in federal funding, the cynics among us might reserve their cheers for a later time. The commitment by Congress of $17.5 million is still only as much as it costs to build four miles of interstate freeway.

Finally the architects, whose marks on paper are the final signature declaring a building's birth or death, are also discovering the new realities of their profession. As late in the game as November of 1977, one of the more progressive architecture magazines asked the incredulous question, "Is Preservation Pop?" The editor was astonished to discover what preservationists had known for years—yes indeed, conservation of old structures is now considered part of the mainstream of popular thinking. In fact, a recent survey by the same magazine discovered that 87.6 per cent of the nation's private architecture firms will be involved in remodeling projects during 1977–78. The firms sampled reported that over one third of their total volume will be concerned with remodeling projects, as compared with only one fifth in 1975.

Suburbs, the Future Slums?

Urban preservationists must have finally gained the attention of the public because now even our political leaders are concerned. National leaders are now exclaiming, "The slums of the future are in the suburbs. . . . The poor always end up in most undesirable areas. Many will be forced into the cheaply built subdivisions thrown up after World War II—the matchbox-like, poorly insulated housing the middle class will desert. . . .

To some, this building has no value. It has been abandoned, burned. Yet it stands, waiting. Is there someone left who is not blind to its beauty?

You'll see the suburbs trying to annex their center cities."

If you are a battle-scarred restorer of old houses in some abandoned center-city neighborhood, the above comments will seem especially ironic. Permit yourself a small smile of triumph as you mutter "I told you so" under your breath. This is exactly what you have been telling the politicians, the planners, the architects, the bankers, for years. Now, as usual, everyone is overreacting to the sudden realization that old neighborhoods and old buildings are indeed attractive and valuable. The people with the suburban mentality now fear that they will reap the whirlwind which they caused with their neglect of those same buildings and neighborhoods many years ago. After trying to flee from the problems of the city, which are in reality the basic problems of life, and now finding those same problems standing outside your suburban split-level—where do you run?

Hopefully, deteriorating suburbs and restoring cities can live in mutual harmony. Not everybody appreciates the closeness and variety of city life. Because of increasing population, the nation is expected to build more structures in the next quarter century than all of what we have built to date. The return to the city, the conservation of old urban buildings and neighborhoods, can be a positive, long-term contribution to an improved American quality of life. But this can only be accomplished if good sense and sensitivity go into the planning and preservation process.

The following chapters will deal with some of the basic "how tos" of urban preservation. America is poised at the threshold of its last and most challenging frontier—the rebirth of its cities. We have come full circle since the Pilgrims first landed on the frigid shores of Massachusetts. We have conquered every wilderness that America holds. There are only two left; the wilderness of our vacant, vandalized urban spaces and the wilderness of a nation's spirit which made them that way. Their conquest could be the greatest victory of all.

Behind this 1950s misguided improvement, there is another door. The rewards of preservation are found in always looking for the other door to history, to priceless architecture hidden behind the walls of neglect.

How to Come Back to the City —and Stay

The city isn't for everyone, especially a city neighborhood which has been deteriorating for several decades. Or for that matter, any old house, whether it is a New York brownstone, a Queen Anne in Galveston, or a rural Carpenter's Frenzy, poses special challenges for which most of us aren't prepared.

We have been carefully taught by a half century of advertising that old things should be discarded for the new model. Even our cities could be discarded with their refuse of the poor, the old, the ones who couldn't quite catch the American Dream Express as it chugged off to Suburban Heaven.

But some people are getting off the train. They are a special kind of person. Whether they are the pioneer who is returning to the city, or one who is struggling to remain in the city, they have developed a unique attitude about themselves and their environment.

The urban pioneer is an elitist, but one far different than what most outsiders think. As the preceding examples of preservation activity around America suggest, the "elite" preservationist comes in every age, race, color, sex, and economic category known to man. But what differentiates this kind of citizen from all the others are these special characteristics: *imagination* to be able to see the potential goodness in a building and a neighborhood which the majority have con-

Preservationists in the Historic Hill District of Saint Paul have learned to work together for everyone's gain. Whether it is salvaging old-house parts from city-condemned buildings or helping a friend sheetrock his living room, it's always better when it is done together.

demned and discarded . . . the *creativity* to take
a devalued piece of property and to sculpt it into
something attractive and worthy . . . the *self-
confidence* to decide that he can do it by himself
in spite of a majority opinion that says it can't
be done . . . the *courage* to move in, or stay in,
a neighborhood where all the statistics of crime,
deterioration, health, and neglect tell him to go
away . . . the sheer *stubbornness* to prove that
the impossible can be accomplished in spite of
the supercilious smiles of suburban friends, local
politicians, bankers, real estate agents, and probably several astonished relatives. In addition,
many battle-scarred old-house restorers, over a
late-night cup of coffee while patching holes or
scraping paint, may suggest that it also helps if
you are a little bit crazy.

*Mrs. Bridler of Mobile has restored almost an entire
block of houses in her De Tonti Square neighborhood. Nobody else would do it, she said, so she just
did it herself.*

One of the earliest pioneers in the Society Hill
district of Philadelphia asserts that a person has
to be mean and fierce and suspicious in order to
be a successful preservationist. A lady in Mobile,
who has battled unsympathetic city councilmen
for decades, agrees and says if you want anything
done to improve your neighborhood, you might
as well do it yourself. A rehabber in Harlem says
that sometimes you do it out of sheer desperation
but, praise the Lord, once you set your mind to
do it, it gets done.

And, finally, it helps if the urban pioneer just
naturally likes people. A loft dweller in Boston
described the difference between the suburbanite
and the urban preservationist as the difference
between a solitary homesteader and a barn raiser.
Preservationists like to get together for recreation
as well as self-help and self-protection. They are
the Pilgrims and pioneer come full circle, learning to do it themselves or do without, dealing
with the universal unsolved cataclysms of crime,
poverty, deterioration on their own block in order
to find personal solutions for them. The single
conclusion which every preservationist finally
comes to is this: Work goes easier when you're
working together, problems go away when you're
talking together, but in the end things get done
by one's own personal commitment.

An Investment of Emotion

Of course, there are solid economic reasons
for restoring old buildings. But almost every
preservationist who was asked why he bought
that particular old house would reply, "Because
I liked it." People often talk about an old house
as if it were a lover, or a lost waif that needed
comforting. A San Francisco couple said that
when they first saw their house in all its dirt and
shabbiness, they wanted to throw their arms
around it. They wanted it, right then and there,
no matter how bad it looked or what it cost.
People need passion in their lives; they need
something on which to focus themselves.

A house is like a sculpture, something to be
molded and cared for and admired. A house need
not be just something in which one eats and sleeps
and goes to the bathroom. A house can be an ex-

To some people, deteriorated old houses are like a work of art. The beauty is there. It is up to you to help it shine through for you and the world to see.

It takes a special kind of person to see beauty in a burned-out, abandoned building. But preservationists in Charleston saw the potential and realized it as these before and after photos prove. (Photos courtesy Historic Charleston Foundation and Louis Schwartz.)

tension of oneself, a flag to fly to tell the world where you are and who you are. Restoring an old building is a means of communicating, a means of asserting oneself, a means of reaching out to others.

When someone asked Louis Armstrong to explain what jazz music is, he replied, "If you have to ask what jazz is, you'll never know." The same thing seems to be true with restoring old houses and old neighborhoods. Not everyone gets an ecstatic emotional reaction when confronted with an old building. In fact, the reaction is most likely one of aversion and disgust. We educated out of ourselves a long time ago any sensitivity to an appreciation of old dormers, cornices, gambrels, and beveled glass.

But some people do get turned on by the thought of investing a few years, or a lifetime, in restoring a structure someone else discarded or misused. This book speaks to those people, the minority of Americans who have somehow acquired a new kind of "elitist" attitude—an emotional response to an old object and old values, a commitment to accomplish a task which most people find neither worthy nor rewarding. Yet the pioneer goes his or her way in spite of popular opinion, finding rewards people didn't know even existed. There are few cities in America where this old attitude remains. But there is one city which especially proves that the modern urban pioneer is not traveling a solitary path.

Charleston: Where Preservation Is a Way of Life

Charleston, South Carolina, is unique in American cities because the love of old houses and the appreciation of urban living was not educated out of its citizens. In spite of hurricanes, devastating fires, and intensive bombardment in both the Revolutionary and Civil wars, Charleston remains today the best-preserved Colonial city in America. There is no other city in America that is so alive and well, so intact and well preserved.

Of course, Charleston fell on hard times after the Civil War and again after World War I. Many people were poor, and many old buildings were neglected. Yet, most of the residents continued to live in the city. And when prosperity returned, the citizens rejected any thought of the traditional knockdown form of urban renewal. Instead, they enacted America's first "historic zone" ordinance in 1931. They also created one of the first architectural review boards in the nation, to control exterior building alterations and site improvements.

Not one but two resident-controlled preservation groups were formed—the Save Charleston Foundation and the Historic Charleston Society—to lead early attempts in developing laws and techniques for the restoration of the community. The result has been not a self-conscious museum of seventeenth- and eighteenth-century houses but a lively, eminently livable city. And the restoration movement goes on today, spreading out from the center-city residential core to the surrounding neighborhoods which were eighteenth- and nineteenth-century suburbs of the city.

When asked why Charleston was able to preserve its past while most American cities did not, Greg Paxton, associate director of the Historic Charleston Foundation, replied that Charlestonians have a long sense of tradition and a healthy respect for their buildings. A sophisticated social life developed in the community early, and despite wars and financial reverses, residents have held on to their sense of physical identity and social responsibility. Even the disrupting influences of new prosperity and federal promises of renewal funding did not shake their appreciation for their architectural and historic heritage.

Even in the sensitive area of downtown business revitalization, the citizens of Charleston are taking a clearheaded preservationist approach. An independent Revitalization Office has been formed which reports directly to the mayor. Property owners are encouraged to rehabilitate their old buildings and to intensify their use by upgrading stores and shops on the first floors, developing office space on the second floors, and creating residential space on the upper floors. A small, one-block multi-use commercial center is being built in the center of town, but only after careful input from city residents as to the scale of the new construction and its compatibility with surrounding historic architecture.

The biggest problem that this city of 70,000 seems to have is the pressure of visitors who come to stand in awe at this almost perfectly preserved and beautifully working community. One is constantly amazed that families still live and work in these gems of Colonial and Federal architecture. Life goes on as it has for over three hundred years. The economy of the city is enormously healthy, in large part due to tourism. People come from every part of America to admire what their own communities have discarded as worthless many years ago. The people of Charleston still get turned on by old buildings every day of their lives. Some of us are only beginning to relearn what they knew all along.

Is Preservation "Economically Feasible?"

What is an old house worth? Can restoration and re-use pass the sharp-penciled scrutiny of an accountant who was weaned on the milk of profits from new construction?

We have come a long way since the Mount Vernon Ladies Association became the first American preservationists by saving George Washington's home in 1853. Since then, and up until recently, it was the ladies, bless them, who led the battle for historic preservation. The men were too busy making money and planning progress to become involved in the little old ladies' recreation of the nonprofit salvation of history. Preservation was something that only maiden aunts and retired ministers could afford to do because profit, the grease that makes American economy roll, was not in it.

There will always be a need for the house museum, the nonprofit restoration project to be used primarily for its educational and aesthetic value. But today, because of limited natural resources and rising prices, the often impractical concept of pure restoration has been transformed into recycled history with historic preservation becoming the more populist form of conservation. Preservation then begins to pay in hard cash as well as good feelings.

Preservation has come out of the little old ladies' closet by becoming profitable, the only language most politicians, chambers of com-

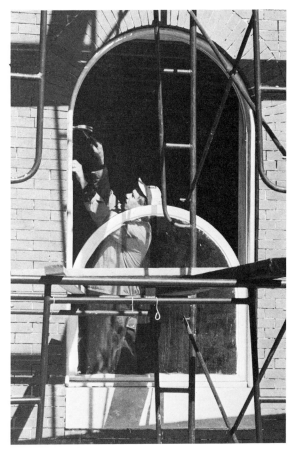

Preservation pays. It means more jobs, better housing, lower taxes, energy saved, less pollution, urban centers that are alive and attractive again.

merce, and bankers understand. The old-house enthusiast need no longer apologize for his emotional attachment to a scruffy old building, because beneath the dirt and disrepair lies a darned good investment.

And because of it, Pulaski Square in Savannah is revitalized; twenty-nine large savings and loan associations created a joint loan pool to finance property improvements in Cincinnati's Madisonville district; the worst slum area in the city has been transformed into St. Paul's Historic Hill District; and neighborhoods from Portland, Oregon, to Portland, Maine, which had been given up for lost, are now the brightest and busiest places in town.

This sharp shift in American consciousness has been brought about by a basic change in the traditional concept of what constitutes an old building. Previously, it was thought of as a debit to social and economic progress. After a certain number of years, dictated by insurance statistical tables, it was literally "written off" because it had exhausted its apparent worth, leaving no other value to the property than that of the land beneath it. This then became its assessed value.

When building inspectors viewed an old building, they literally did not see it. They only saw the need to make it a "new" structure in order to meet the health and safety standards which were computed for new construction. Financial institutions also did not see the old structure as an essential value to the land beneath it, but only what new structure could be built on the cleared land to give it "the highest and best use."

An old house is a partially complete new house.

One person who has led the effort to change our economic consciousness about old buildings has been Arthur Skolnik, former district manager of the Pioneer Square Historic District in Seattle. He proved that good aesthetics, good sociology, and good planning make good economic sense when united with old architecture.

In the early 1970s, Seattle was in a deep recession. But at the insistence of people like Skolnik,

"In-place value," the true value of an old structure, can revolutionize the conservation movement. Art Skolnik has used this concept to help restore Seattle's Pioneer Square. Now he is taking the message to other communities.

the city invested in such supposed frills as old buildings, an old market, parks, and trees. Hitchhiking on the record of a few people who had personally restored old buildings in the Pioneer Square area, a local public expenditure of several hundred thousand dollars was matched by a couple of million dollars in federal, state, and foundation grants. This was accomplished in spite of the protests of many local businessmen who said fixing up old structures was just throwing good money after bad. But these expenditures eventually catalyzed millions of dollars in expanded private redevelopment of buildings and shops to bring into the area new residents and thousands of money-spending visitors. This, in turn, caused an over 1,000 per cent increase in the Pioneer Square district's tax base between 1970 and 1975. Partly because of this imaginative re-use of its history, *Harper's* magazine in 1974 declared Seattle to be the most "liveable" city in America. In 1977, *New West* magazine repeated the compliment.

Seattle's transformation came about partly because of a change in thinking regarding old structures. Skolnik suggests that the old assessed value of an elderly structure should be changed to a conservation-oriented concept of "in-place value." The in-place value is vastly greater than its assessed value because the usual assessor uses outmoded criteria that down-value the real value of the structure. He is usually concerned only with the traditional demolition value of used bricks, et cetera, and the immediate value or negative value of the surrounding deteriorated structures in a slum neighborhood.

But the in-place value causes one to view an old building, no matter how deteriorated, as a partially completed new structure. There is an intrinsic economic value in the existing utilities provided to the site, the value of existing studs, foundation, bricks, materials, special architectural details, and the like. What essentially happens in the "highest and best use" new building construction concept is first the old structure is demolished, bricks hauled away, and so forth. Then new bricks and materials are hauled in and another structure erected. The in-place value suggests elimination of the costly and time-consuming middle-man step of demolition and new construction.

Even the most deteriorated building still contains an in-place value of $10 per square foot, Skolnik estimates. Developers and politicians should be educated to see the economic feasibility of not wasting $10 per square foot of millions of square feet of deteriorated floor space in almost every city, multiplied by nearly five million structures, in all urban areas of America, which are in need of rehabilitation or threatened with demolition.

The actual "hard costs" of restoring an old building, including not having to demolish it in the first place, have been estimated by a San Francisco developer to be 40 to 50 per cent of

Sweat equity is the economic foundation of most preservation projects. Maybe the job doesn't get done quite as fast, but it is accomplished to your satisfaction. Especially when you are young; it's easier to pay the bill in hours than in dollars.

the cost of constructing a new building. In addition, there is a big saving in the "soft costs," such as insurance and tax expenditures during the construction, because restoration construction time is usually shorter. Interim financing is also less.

These soft-cost savings alone can reduce the total package for permanent financing on a commercial project by $12 a rentable square foot less than it would be for new construction. And, frequently, because restoration work does not have to shut down the entire building, an income stream from current tenants can be maintained during renovation, further reducing the long-term financing.

The National Economic Feasibility of Preservation

The profitability of preservation for the private developer is one strong argument for saving old buildings. The social values of keeping a neighborhood stable and preserving the identity of a community through conservation instead of demolition is another. And even more important are the national implications of preservation. A Housing and Urban Development study recently concluded that recycling our cities instead of building new suburbs may consume 50 per cent less land, 55 per cent less capital, 45 per cent less energy, and create 45 per cent less air pollution. For example, in 1982, if the rehabilitation movement increased from 32 per cent to 39 per cent of the total national construction market, with a resulting decrease in new construction, the energy saved would equal a saving of 30 million barrels of crude oil for the year. That is enough to provide all the energy needed for 800,000 households for the year. If the preservation share of the market were increased from 39 per cent to 46 per cent, there would be a resultant saving of 60 million barrels of crude oil, enough to provide the total energy needs for 1.6 million houses for a year.

In addition, rehabilitation projects are heavily labor intensive, with often 75 per cent of the dollars expended for labor costs. New construction is usually about 50 per cent labor and 50 per cent materials. So, money invested in rehabilitation goes directly into the local economy to provide more jobs and to support local businesses.

Is our business-minded and economy-minded public getting the message? It appears so, because recent government figures show that rehabilitation, also known as repair and alteration or renovation, for nonresidential buildings alone, has grown from 13.5 per cent in 1970 to 21.5 per cent in 1975 and is projected to reach 24.8 per cent in 1977. This will represent nearly $19.9 billion of construction. The rehabilitation of residential property may reach 38 per cent of that market, adding another $32 billion to the construction economy.

What Does It Mean for You?

But what about you? How economically feasible would it be for you to find an old house or commercial building and restore it? It takes a special kind of person, as was indicated in the previous chapter. If you are that kind of person, then the next step is to select a building that appeals to you, in a neighborhood that has some potential for revitalization. These decisions must

The Old Otterbein neighborhood in Baltimore has been described as the largest single urban homesteading site in the nation. Almost one hundred abandoned "$1.00 dwellings" have been reclaimed from blight and decay by both old and new residents of the city.

OTTERBEIN
a Homesteading Community
in
Inner
Harbor
West

OTTERBEIN
COMMUNITY   ASSOCIATION

William Donald Schaefer, May

Thanks to revolving-loan funds, buildings which may have faced demolition are now held for new owners who are willing to restore the structures.

be made through your own perception, courage, and pocketbook.

Historic preservation areas can usually be rated on a scale of one to four. The first stage is one of *abandonment*. The community's attitude is usually one of total lack of self-pride, self-confidence, and the respect of the larger city community. Buildings have been on the market for years but still have not been sold. Most structures are not owner occupied. Large homes may sell for a few thousand dollars. Commercial property stands vacant. Residents' sense of hopelessness is expressed in crime and neglect. Restoring a building in this environment takes the greatest amount of courage and energy, but could require the least amount of money.

Stage Two is a neighborhood which shows *pockets of pride*. One or more structures on a block may be in the process of rehabilitation. One or two young couples may be seen working on their home or storefront. Maybe one or two news items appear in the local paper referring to positive things happening in the neighborhood, instead of just the usual crime statistics. At this stage, absentee landlords may be aware of some renewal potential, so the fourteen-room house you may have bought in Stage One for $6,000 now costs $12,000.

Stage Three is the *restoration* phase. A neighborhood association has been formed. Maybe half of the structures in the neighborhood have new owners and new paint jobs. Local real estate people are tentatively driving by, wondering whether they have found a new market. The deteriorated fourteen-room house, still in the same condition as Stage One, is now for sale at $24,000.

Stage Four is the *respectable* phase. The president of the neighborhood association is now on a first-name basis with the mayor. A councilman or two may have bought a home or a building in the community. Ninety per cent of the buildings have been restored, half with period interiors and half with stainless-steel kitchen chairs and pop art. Middle-aged couples from the suburbs are purchasing already restored houses from the original preservationists. Residents are complaining about the overcommercialism of the neighborhood. The same fourteen-room house now sells for $48,000 unrestored, $90,000 to $225,-000 restored.

The Ripple Effect

In many cities, the restoration of one house or one block can create a geometric progression of old-house restoration which looks like the ripples made on a clear pond when one stone is dropped. A public consciousness arises, hopefully fostered by newspaper articles and strong neighborhood publicity, which can renew an entire city.

If you don't have the courage to be the initial restoration pioneer and don't have the cash to jump in at stages Three or Four of a restoring neighborhood, look around at the surrounding deteriorated neighborhoods. If the quality of architecture is good, and if the area's landmarks and amenities have potential for improvement, this neighborhood may be ripe for a Stage Two beginning. If you like the building, buy it. Your restoring of it could be the drop of the pebble needed to cause the ripple effect in your neighborhood.

In order to foster a development of pride in your block, you may wish to plan your improvements to enhance the process. First, of course, you must secure the building from further deterioration: you might replace the roof, fix the heating plant, make sure that a third-floor water pipe is not about to burst. Then celebrate the street and startle your neighbors with a highly visible exterior restoration. Maybe you should paint the exterior as authentically and tastefully as possible, or tear off the misguided improvement of the 1950s fake-brick front porch, or clean up the front yard and plant flowers. Let people know that there is a new kid on the block and you're here to stay.

After that, surprising things happen. Older residents who may have been intimidated by the slow deterioration of the neighborhood may paint their own houses. Young couples looking for a Phase Two or Three neighborhood may decide that yours is the one for them. And it also often brings the change of attitude needed from your banker, policeman, and insurance agent. Your commitment to your neighborhood has made a difference, often multiplied tenfold by the hopes and expectations of others.

Where to Get the Money

Rome wasn't built in a day. And neither will be your neighborhood. Part of the final long-term success of a restored home and its neighborhood seems to lie in the slow, painful, patient, preservation process. Overnight successes never seem to last (more about this in the chapter "Looking Beyond Preservation").

So make big plans and long-range plans for restoring your home. Enjoy the pain and pleasure of doing a lot of the work yourself, both in order to keep costs down and also to enjoy the satisfaction of re-creating a quality structure which only manual toil seems to bring. As misery loves company, so does the preservation process create a stronger neighborhood-friendship and mutual-help bond among neighbors.

One of the main topics of conversation at any old-house-community cocktail party is financing, or how can I afford a new furnace before winter comes? There is no one way to finance the ownership and restoration of an old building, but here is a list of possible sources of funding which may help fit your particular needs.

1. Sweat Equity—No matter how wealthy the prospective preservationist is, this is one ingredient which should be in every financing mixture. Without it, preservation isn't half the fun. As was mentioned earlier, approximately 75 per cent of the costs for restoring a building are labor costs. How much of that labor is yours and how much of it is someone else's can dictate what your final rehabilitation bill will be.

2. Urban Homesteading—Some cities have implemented urban homesteading programs, a method of recycling abandoned inner-city buildings. In New York City, abandoned multiple-unit dwellings in severely deteriorated neighborhoods are being changed to sound housing through the labor of previously unemployed community residents. By contributing sweat equity, the home-

steaders become the owners of their own building through a co-operative purchase agreement.

In Baltimore, the city sells vacant houses for $1.00 each, on the condition that the buyer move in within six months of purchase and bring the building up to code standards within two years. City property taxes are waived during the initial period and loans of up to twenty years are made available at low interest rates. Many other cities such as Minneapolis and Philadelphia have developed similar programs.

3. Conventional Mortgages—Local banks and savings and loan institutions have been notorious for their lack of enthusiasm about making loans in poor areas of the city. Only recently have their "redlining" practices been changed to allow some inner-city home-buying and restoration loans to be purchased.

In order to encourage the financial institutions to provide loans to previously redlined areas, some cities and states are guaranteeing the loans for the banks. Also, some federal backing is also available. For example, the Federal Housing Administration-insured Title 1 Home Improvement Loan Program now insures bank loans for persons improving properties listed in the National Register of Historic Places.

The best advice for the preservationist is to get to know your local banker. And then present him with a complete and professional-looking loan application. Note Richard Crissman's Ideal Loan Application.

4. Revolving Loan Funds—One of the earliest revolving funds to finance historic preservation occurred in Savannah during the 1950s when the Historic Savannah Foundation, Inc., raised private money to purchase run-down old buildings and resell them for restoration, sometimes at a loss. Income resulting from these transactions is then returned to the fund to be used again. Several preservation organizations around the nation are using this financing method for both purchase and rehabilitation of deteriorated buildings. Some municipalities, such as the city of Seattle, are also using the revolving loan fund concept.

5. Tax Incentives—The Tax Reform Act of 1976 provides major tax incentives for rehabilitation

by owners of commercial or income-producing historic structures, and tax penalties for those who demolish such structures. (See "How to Gain Control" chapter.)

Several states and cities have also passed legislation either providing tax exemptions for certain historic properties or have provided tax moratoriums for improvements made to old structures. Check with your local governmental body to see if you have this type of progressive tax legislation. If not, lobby to make sure that the old-house owner has at least the same benefits as the new-house owner.

6. The Urban Reinvestment Task Force—Through the Task Force's Neighborhood Housing Services program, neighborhood partnerships are set up between the residents, the private sector, and the local government. These partnerships are provided technical assistance and receive Task Force grants which are used to create high-risk revolving loan funds which stimulate lending by financial institutions. Grants are also available for the Task Force's Neighborhood Preservation Projects program. These grants are made to existing neighborhood programs for specific projects which, if successful, might provide useful models for other neighborhoods.

7. Tax Increment Financing—A technique for over-all neighborhood improvement, property taxes are collected above a designated amount in a particular district and set aside for use only within that designated area. Money can immediately pay for any special needs of the area or can be invested for future use. California, Minnesota, and Colorado have state enabling legislation for this preservation concept.

8. Other Funding Sources—There are several publications which preservationists can consult for information on preservation funding. The National Trust for Historic Preservation has published *A Guide to Federal Programs* which provides a comprehensive survey of federal programs that can be used to benefit preservation. Probable sources include: Veterans Administration, Farmers Home, Small Business Administration, National Endowment, etc. Available through the National Trust Bookstore, 740–748 Jackson

Place, N.W., Washington, D.C. 20006. Another publication, *Federal Programs for Neighborhood Conservation* can be ordered from the Advisory Council on Historic Preservation, 1522 K Street, N.W., Suite 430, Washington, D.C. 20005. Also see "Getting Started" chapter in this book.

THE IDEAL LOAN APPLICATION

The perfect application is the one which is approved by the lender. The approach to such perfection is easier when documents are arranged to answer the lender's need to know the sources of debt coverage, equity, and credit. (*Courtesy Richard Crissman*).

	TYPES OF LOANS		
	Commercial	Apartment	*Home and* Condominium
1. Items defining the scope of the project for the lender (what, where, by whom, and how much):			
Brief description of the project	×	×	×
Area photos	×	×	×
City map showing project location	×	×	×
Key floor plan	×	×	×
Plat map (as from title report)	×	×	×
2. Items relating to lender's debt-service measurements:			
Schedule of income and expenses	×	×	
Schedule of competing rentals	×	×	
Map of competing rentals	×	×	
Market study with comparable sales			×
Map of comparable sales			×
Summary of committed tenants (rates)	×		
Summary of declared buyers (prices)			×
3. Items relating to lender's measure of equity (and ability to finish the project):			
Purchase documentation	×	×	×
Alteration drawings	×	×	×
Alteration building permit	×	×	×
Engineering, soils, seismic studies	×	×	×
Specifications and material lists	×	×	×
Cost breakdown, signed	×	×	×
Building contract, signed (subject to loan funding)	×	×	×
Appraisal	×	×	×

	Types of Loans		
			Home and
	Commercial	Apartment	Condominium
4. Items relating to developer's ability and willingness to pay:			
Developer's background and capabilities	×	×	×
Financial statement (balance sheet)	×	×	×
Cash-flow projection, this project	×	×	×
Credit report (or authorization)	×	×	×
5. Items relating to tenant's or home buyer's ability to pay:			
Annual reports	×		
Credit report (or authorization)			×
Financial statements of buyers			×
Deposit receipts			×
Letters of intent to lease	×	×	

How to Organize for Self-Preservation

One person attempting to fight city hall is a complainer. One hundred is a constituency. Nothing is more lonely and futile than to try to take on singlehandedly either a recalcitrant city council or a deteriorating neighborhood. There is strength in numbers. There is security in numbers. There is preservation success in numbers.

Although we often emphasize buildings when thinking of historic preservation, let us never forget that a group of buildings make up a "neighborhood," and neighborhoods are people. The only difference between a good and bad neighborhood, as Jane Jacobs expressed in her classic book *The Death and Life of Great American Cities,* is how much its people care about it. She said, "Our failures with city neighborhoods are, ultimately, failure in localized self-government—both the informal and formal self-management of society."

Philosopher Reinhold Niebuhr scoffed at people who try to justify good shelter on grounds that it will work social miracles. He called such efforts "the doctrine of salvation by bricks." I contend that united concern for old buildings, community history, and good housing can work social and economic miracles. The physical revitalization process of stages One through Four listed in the previous chapter is really a communication process, a neighborhood organizational process. Depending on the degree to which

Preservation is people and their commitment to being involved in the ongoing community-revitalization process. It is the preservation organizations' responsibility to help individuals make that commitment. (Photo courtesy Old Town Restorations, Inc. and James Wengler.)

everyone in the community is involved in that process, then salvation by bricks can indeed mean the salvation of the people, both rich and poor. "Displacement" usually occurs because the degree of community organization and representation has been faulty.

If this book serves no other purpose, I hope that it reveals the marvelous assortment of people behind the equally marvelous restored buildings all over America. During the last few years, we have moved light-years away from the traditional concept of historic preservation as the house museum, with the ladies' aid societies going begging hat-in-hand to male businessmen for a few dollars to save it as a sort of Uncle Tom house while progress demolishes everything else around it.

Today, old buildings and old neighborhoods can no longer be thought of as archaic stumbling blocks to progress. In a growing number of cases all across the nation, public officials who still think this way soon find themselves out of a job.

Not surprisingly, this basic transformation in American society has not come from our public leaders or so-called housing experts. Urban planning and the abomination of 1950s urban renewal evolved out of our civil engineers and architects who used our cities as an overgrown demolition derby with the rules of the game decreeing our environment to be expendable. They forgot that part of the environment is people, and it was finally only through outrage at the gross trashing of their neighborhoods that the people responded.

In almost every American city and town, the new phenomenon of neighborhood conservation has grown like a mighty oak from the slender sapling of museum-type historic restoration. The house museum, the isolated restored building, was the critical first step from which has grown the larger concept of saving the *tout ensemble*—the entire relationship of a neighborhood of structures. And the success of each community's efforts rests on the success of the organization behind it; an organization usually of "nonexperts," private individuals, who are creating a new political and economic consciousness much like the New England town meetings of old.

Pittsburgh: A New Dimension to Historic Preservation

In 1964 Arthur P. Ziegler, Jr., an English teacher, and James D. Van Trump, an architectural historian, were walking along Liverpool Street on their way to a meeting. They had learned that this slowly deteriorating neighborhood of Manchester and the entire North Side of Pittsburgh were slated for demolition in the name of urban renewal. They decided that if nobody else was

Arthur Ziegler sees his Station Square project as a natural extension of a preservation organization's responsibility of not just restoring old buildings but also proving that the saving of old buildings can make a significant, positive economic impact on the community.

going to save these streets of Italianate, Queen Anne, and Federal buildings, they would.

From their determination grew the Pittsburgh History and Landmarks Foundation; with 2,500 members it is one of the largest community-based preservation organizations in the nation. In determination, innovativeness, and city-wide concern, it may well be the most significant anywhere.

Ziegler is still the leader of this organization, whose list of trustees reads like the "Who's Who" of Pittsburgh's important people as well as a cross section of community residents. He has been called the prophet of preservation for the poor and has probably done more than anyone else to change the tide of historic preservation in this country from concern for just buildings to an equal concern for buildings and the people who reside in them.

The Pittsburgh History and Landmarks Foundation (PHLF) has today largely turned around the intent of their former foe, the Pittsburgh Urban Redevelopment Authority. By working with city government and the URA, Ziegler has developed a truly amazing restoration program for the threatened Manchester area. The URA is now selling abandoned houses for $100 to $9,000. It will then pay the new or present owner 10 per cent of the building's appraised value for a façade easement. The URA will then restore the façade at no cost if the owner agrees to maintain the restored façade for twenty years. The URA also offers free specs, bids, drawings, construction supervision, and 3 per cent loans to do the interior rehabilitation. If you're poor, the city will give you an outright grant.

Ziegler's Landmarks organization is in charge of an $85,000 annual budget for marketing this program. In their first attempt, they had a meeting of eight hundred residents and sold fifty houses within seventy-two hours. They are now going public with professionally produced television and newspaper advertising.

As you may surmise, Ziegler is the head of no ordinary preservation organization. He is involved in several programs to save fifteen declining Pittsburgh neighborhoods in which some 75,000 persons live.

The Mexican War Street neighborhood has become the first mixed-income, integrated preservation district in the county. The great amount of publicity generated by this program, which included low-interest loans and free design help, was a key event in developing more of a social conscience for preservation efforts everywhere in the United States. The economic results were satisfying, too, with PHLF and the city spending $450,000 to spur a private expenditure in restoration of $3 million.

Ziegler and his organization in 1967 created a small beautification program in Birmingham, a South Side blue-collar neighborhood. This led from residents planting window boxes of flowers, to cleaning streets and vacant lots, to fixing up their houses. Then PHLF convinced a group of local financial institutions to create a high-risk rehabilitation loan fund which grew to $1 million. This, in turn, led to the creation by the federal government of Neighborhood Housing Services, a public-private neighborhood revitalization program which is being used in many cities across the nation.

One of Ziegler's most recent and spectacular preservation projects is Station Square—the restoration and re-use of forty acres of railroad buildings on Pittsburgh's South Side. What was a railroad terminal, express house, freight house, seven-story warehouse and six-story office building will become the largest recycling project in the nation, according to *Business Week* magazine. At the cost of $30 million, a mixed-use center containing the largest restaurant in Pittsburgh, 100 shops and other restaurants, 360,000 square feet of office space, parking for 2,200 cars, and a new 250-room hotel will rise. It's the largest renewal project in the history of the city, the third largest concentration of office space outside the central business district, will employ four thousand people in the first phase of development, will have projected annual sales of $28 million a year or 25 per cent of Pittsburgh's retail sales. And Ziegler's staff of eighteen people is handling all design, construction management, promotion, advertising, graphics, and leasing for the $30-million project. The little old ladies in tennis shoes have come a long way.

Ziegler received initial funding of $5 million for the project from the Allegheny Foundation which is a trust of Pittsburgh's Scaife family. The

The Birmingham neighborhood on Pittsburgh's South Side has the longest (nineteen blocks) Victorian commercial street in America. PHLF has developed a marketing program which by 1977 had leased twenty-one new shops in the many vacant commercial buildings.

Scaifes and other local foundations have been the main source of support for the Pittsburgh History and Landmarks Foundation. Not surprisingly, although the city is the third largest corporate headquarters in the United States, local corporations' interest in Ziegler's revitalization activities has been minimal. Businesses still see Ziegler's form of urban revitalization as either competition or they are unable to place him in the usual niches of other "social service" agencies. When he calls, they say, "We gave to the United Fund."

Businessmen were even more surprised to learn that the net income from this mammoth Station Square commercial complex will go into a fund for the continuing restoration of Pittsburgh's inner-city neighborhoods. It will be the first possibility of long-range funding that the PHLF has had.

You should be willing to risk everything, every day of your life.

Ziegler is an extraordinary person, a man who makes million-dollar decisions on weekdays and then recruits local children on Sundays to cut the grass around the Foundation's restored Old Post Office headquarters. Yet almost every successful preservation organization across the nation must have at least one person like Ziegler. They have to, in order to survive. How else can we explain the extraordinary feats of so many groups of uninitiated, untrained, unfunded people who have accomplished more in the area of urban revitalization than have all the federal urban renewal programs in the country which had access to the nation's greatest experts, political backing, and funding?

What Arthur Ziegler, Jr., has, and dozens of other men and women have who make the preservation movement what it is today, is the ability to make a deep and emotional commitment to preserving old buildings and old neighborhoods, and then is able to transmit that commitment to others. It is the ability to be innovative, to take risks aggressively.

Ziegler says that a preservation leader has to run his organization with the willingness to go out of business tomorrow if he can't make it. As soon as he or she decides to play it safe and starts hiring a lot of consultants to remove the burden of decision-making from his shoulders, he is done for. If an organization sees what can be done and believes in it, and assumes the responsibility, it can do tremendous things. You've just got to get out and do it.

Doing it was easier when a famous person's old house was about to be demolished for a parking lot, even though this "easier" early phase of preservation has its horror stories to tell. But it is many times more complicated and difficult now when the restoration problem is the block, the neighborhood, the city where you live. Then, the "doing it" calls for highly sophisticated communications and organizational ability.

The challenging element of historic and neighborhood preservation in America is its diversity. There is no one type of preservation problem, no one kind of solution, and no one way for an organization to accomplish it. But each preservation organization, whether it is a block or neighborhood group, a community landmark foundation, or a city-wide association of preservation organizations, is involved with similar organizational dynamics. Here is a brief outline of those dynamics which may help you create your own organization or may help you improve the effectiveness of the one you already have.

Organizing: How to Do It

1. The Catalyst: Almost every preservation organization grew out of a crisis—a key historic building about to be demolished, a freeway about to decimate a community, urban renewal about to demolish a neighborhood. Today there is also a new type of catalyst which does not wait for a crisis to happen. Some communities are forward-looking enough to be concerned about and begin to organize *conservation districts,* those neighborhoods which aren't yet threatened but need to be nurtured through their old age. In either case, it is important to carefully identify what the catalyst is as well as who your enemies and your friends are when dealing with the catalyst.

2. The Leaders: Someone has to feel strongly enough about the catalytic concern to do something about it. One or two or a dozen people are all it takes to begin to make enormous changes. But the most difficult thing in the world is to find that special person, even if he or she should be yourself, who is willing to make a total commitment. To accomplish anything of significance, please note that for a month, a year, or a lifetime, the commitment will have to be almost total for at least one member of the organization's leadership.

As was mentioned earlier, essential credentials of the true leader are passion, dedication, imagination, the courage to take risks, the ability to communicate and organize, patience, and perseverance. The leader need not be an "expert," such as a politician, a planner, an architect, a banker. In fact, it appears that the traditional training for success in the business and professional world often hinders one's ability to be creative and take risks.

Often, help for a deteriorating neighborhood comes from outside, as was the case in Milwaukee's Historic Walkers Point. The mostly suburban members of the Junior League, called "the Ladies of Walkers Point" by the Mexican and Serbian blue-collar residents, have come into the community to help form an increasingly effective neighborhood preservation process.

3. The Constituency: It is difficult for leaders to be successful if they don't have a large, diverse, and passionate following. As you define the catalyst or the "cause," also define who may be affected negatively by the catalytic problem. If the problem is a neighborhood threatened by urban renewal, your constituency may include: (a) every resident in the immediately affected area; (b) residents in other neighborhoods which might be affected in the future; (c) local historical societies, architectural associations, social organizations; (d) local colleges with departments of urban affairs, architecture, history, and geography; (e) sympathetic members of city and state agencies, as well as other preservation organizations.

4. Articulate the Cause: What is the extent of the problem? Who will be affected? What is the magnitude of the loss if cause (i.e., buildings demolished, people left homeless, aesthetic loss, economic loss, historical loss, jobs lost, et cetera) happens negatively? Write your argumentation down as clearly and concisely as possible in a Position Paper so that you can clarify your own thinking as well as persuade others.

Of course, at this time, it is wise to contact the perpetrator of the problem. This could be a private developer, your city council, the Urban Development Authority, or others. Attempt to see if through reasonable and traditional measures the problem can be solved. If this is not possible, go on to Step 5.

5. Initial Organizational Publicity: There is only one way to discover if you indeed have a cause and a constituency, and that is to cry wolf and see who comes running. In some way, you must try to gain your supposed constituents' attention in order to see if and how they will react.

You may wish to stage a confrontation, create a little "street theater" such as organizing a small protest among your friends to block bulldozers or stage a demonstration in city council chambers or any event that may prove newsworthy. Prior to your demonstration, visit your local news media to state your case and invite them to the confrontation. More mundane ways of attracting your constituency's attention may be by simply

Frank Peborsky, a Croatian who has lived in Historic Walkers Point for fifty-eight years, says he likes what the ladies are doing. He even got an award for keeping his house so nice. But the best reward of all is the other people who are also fixing up the old houses around him.

telephoning as many people as possible, passing out flyers and so on. You may also want to accomplish these tasks in conjunction with the above demonstration.

6. The Organizational Meeting: Following the initial publicity, a gathering of the constituency should be called. Suggest a central meeting place, or a series of meetings convenient to most of your constituency. As briefly and graphically as possible, explain what the problem is. Then, provide a period of open discussion to assess the degree of concern and involvement which comes from your audience. This is the key moment: Is there a real universal concern? Will your organization have more working members than just yourself?

7. Incorporating: If you find that you indeed have an enthusiastic constituency behind you, make it official as soon as possible. Have the constituency vote a slate of officers. Select committees to accomplish immediate, achievable responsibilities. Have the constituency decide what kinds of financial and personal contributions each member should make. Have formal letters of incorporation drawn up. Consider becoming a 501(c)(3) nonprofit corporation under the Internal Revenue Code. If you intend to be highly political and expect to do a lot of lobbying, a tax-exempt status may be difficult to acquire.

8. Create an Identity: Now is the time to begin appealing to the larger public of politicians, funding sources, potential supporting groups and individuals. Spend as much creative thought as possible on your organization's name. Is it memorable, responsible-sounding, inclusive of your constituency, descriptive of your cause?

Spend an equal amount of time in creating an attractive, high-quality letterhead for your organization. Every letter you write must make a positive impression on the recipient because that letter may be your best and only representative to him. Does the letterhead show an impressive list of directors? Do you have a well-designed and memorable logotype? Does the paper stock have the look and feel of quality?

9. Communicate: If concern over a letterhead seems a rather silly waste of time during this period of crisis, please remember one thing: The preservation business is essentially a communications business. Deep-held prejudices must be overcome, people must be educated to the respectability of looking at an old building in a different way, a new kind of economic and social philosophy must be expressed as convincingly and eloquently as possible.

Very few old houses and old neighborhoods will be saved if a sensitive educational process is not immediately begun and aimed at friends and foes alike. Emotion isn't enough. Calm reason, careful persuasion, compassionate and responsible understanding must be an integral part of your preservation process.

10. Study the Problem: In most preservation crisis cases, the neighborhood organization is not considered the expert. The expert is always the banker who is redlining, the HUD official who is demolishing, the highway official who is building a freeway through your backyard, the architect who has designed a high-rise where your home is.

You must prove the expert wrong in his own area of expertise, with facts, figures, designs, professional-sounding language. Then, in the eyes of at least some of the decision-makers, you too take on an aura of professional credibility.

One thing you will learn early in the preservation game is that although you may have a strong emotional attachment to old neighborhoods, the banker only understands the balance sheet, the developer only understands net profits, the union leader only understands jobs, and the politician only understands votes. You must speak in their language.

Prepare a design study, an inventory of historic structures, an economic impact study, whatever type of professional and credible scientific argumentation it takes to state your case to the decision-makers who are going to make the difference. If you have experts within your organization who can do this, you are fortunate. If not, contact local colleges to see if such studies could be taken on as class projects or if interested professors would be willing to volunteer some of their time. The same approach can be taken with other experts. If not, you will have to find money to pay for a professional firm to do the studies or you will need to hire a professional for your staff. When all else fails, money talks. To a preservationist, "begging" for money becomes an honorable way of life.

11. Fund Raising: Soliciting money has become a high art in most successful preservation organizations. If you are an accredited "nonprofit," resident-based organization, there are usually several private and public foundations whose sole purpose in life is to give money to organizations such as yours.

The art is to make the foundations believe as strongly as you do that your cause is just and that your organization is the only one able to solve the problem. This art is called "proposal writing," and a member of your organization who can write a persuasive proposal is worth his or her weight in gold. Again, communication is important in contacting the potential foundations, asking them for suggestions as to how you can make your proposals successful, and gathering a list of prestigious people who think you are as good as you believe yourself to be.

Other preservation-oriented funds are now available through federal and local grants (see Economics chapter). Don't be afraid to talk with your local legislators about new funding sources which may soon be available. And as many successful preservation organizations suggest ("We have a lot of parties"), fund-raising and fun-raising parties and events should be a regular occurrence for your organization.

12. Communicate Some More: The education process should never stop. Regular membership meetings, special workshops and seminars on everything from home insulation to controlling elm blight to interior decoration, as well as combined meetings between different neighborhoods or city agencies, should all be planned to enhance the educational process.

Tours have proven to be one of the most effective fund-raising and communication tools for preservation groups. Annual home tours, walking tours, bus tours, and the like, help strangers experience the urban environment which turned you on in the first place.

Newsletters, reports, articles in the city newspapers, special neighborhood newspapers, slide shows—all help change the public image about your cause and your neighborhood. Successful organizations like Greater Portland Landmarks, Inc.; Historic Walkers Point in Milwaukee; Galveston Historical Foundation; the New York Brownstone Association, and others, have all created a growing library of sophisticated communication materials.

13. Well-planned Projects: If your organization is going to be long-lived, it is important to plan for not only the ultimate victory, i.e., "When we stop the freeway." In order to keep your constituency involved through the long haul, and to prepare them for positive action before and after your ultimate goal, plan now for a series of smaller victories.

What are a series of attainable goals which will both strengthen your organization and your community? A neighborhood clean-up program? Purchasing and restoring an abandoned building? Offering free design consulting services to the community? Creating a free tool-lending library? An old-house used-parts store? A rent-a-kid program to help residents fix up their property?

Preservation is a process. It is bigger than even that catalytic crisis which initially caught your attention. It is the process of communication and growth for a person, an organization, a community.

It is the instilling of pride. At one city council meeting, a Pittsburgh councilman was talking about funding for the rehabbing of homes on the city's South Side. An old Polish gentleman who had lived long in this sadly deteriorating area rose painfully to his feet. "Mr. Councilman," he said, "I want to make one thing clear. We are not just rehabbing our homes. We are restoring them."

Once the transforming force of preservation begins, it need never stop. Even though the organizations change, the needs of old houses and old neighborhoods continue. You just need to decide to do it—to organize yourself, your neighborhood. The process that evolves from that initial decision can be more rewarding and far-reaching than you may expect.

Creating a New Identity

A "slum" is a state of mind. The actual deterioration occurs in a community because the members of that community and the people who service it act out a self-fulfilling prophesy of civic suicide.

The change in economic and social status of an area may begin with a brief economic depression, a shift in local industry, a few key businesses or homeowners leaving for any number of reasons. No major actual harm may be done by this event, but like a momentary earthquake, it leaves an uneasiness in the community which can create bad vibrations that lead to an accelerating flood of negative impressions about the area.

A new community image is subtly created which causes decisions to be made that fulfill its emerging negative impressions. Local newspapers begin to play up crime reports, city agencies decide to place public improvements in other areas, banks begin to "redline" the area as a place not to approve loans, real estate agents begin the subtle art of blockbusting by mentioning to area homeowners that now is the time to sell before it is too late, taxi drivers warn customers away from the area, even the police and other public servants often unconsciously project the kind of attitudes which indicate a growing lack of respect and confidence in the neighborhood and its residents.

Specific examples of these negative impressions, resulting from the slum-makers' self-fulfilling prophesies, are distressingly similar in every restoring neighborhood in America. In St. Paul's Historic Hill, a police officer tells a house burglary victim that she should expect to be robbed if she has decided to live in "this part of town." A San Diego visitor interested in exploring the restoring Historic Gas Lamp District is told by a hotel clerk that he should stay out of the area and suggests a nice suburban shopping mall instead. A city council decides that an older residential neighborhood in Milwaukee or St. Louis or Pittsburgh would make a good industrial-park site. Homeowners who wish to rehabilitate their homes are refused improvement loans by local financial institutions with the explanation that their community is not a good financial risk.

The result: innumerable negative impressions build to a fulfillment of the prophesy. The community is "bad"—high crime for the city services, high risk for the city financial institutions, low status for anybody who dares to live there.

Finally, as one frustrated neighborhood leader concludes, "Everybody who can gets the hell out." Public attitude abandons the community, then the residents do, too. The final curtain for a successful civic death wish: a certified, bona fide slum.

How to Dispel the Negative Impressions

Public opinion has created a slum out of a viable community. Public opinion can unslum

The people, yes! Individual education, enthusiasm, commitment are what preservation is all about.

that same community. The reason why the original pioneers came to the old neighborhoods in the first place was probably because they possessed unique geographical amenities: near a natural harbor or communications crossroads, on a high bluff or hill, next to some major cultural or economic activity. Then the original pioneers added to the neighborhood's natural amenities with some man-made amenities of their own: well-built, beautifully designed homes and commercial buildings. They surrounded these buildings with streets and parks and public monuments that further enhanced the amenities for living.

Many of those original amenities may still be there in what is now designated a "slum." They may be neglected or deteriorated, misguided improvements may cover some of them, some may have been totally disfigured or demolished. But the essential attractions are still there, maybe

tarnished like forgotten treasures, but still retaining their original priceless value.

You, the modern urban pioneer, have stumbled upon this treasure-trove of neglected architecture. You want to transform it again into a thriving community with all its historic diversity. But just your opinion of its worth isn't enough. How do you re-educate the politician, the banker, the real estate agent, the taxi driver, the policeman, the suburbanite that historic "downtown" is no longer the "inner city" with all its connotations of grime, hopelessness, and worthlessness?

The answer is to communicate, to celebrate the real amenities your community has, to publicize and certify its potential. The reason why there are a thousand tract houses now on what used to be a rural cow pasture is because some smart developer made people want to live in not a cow pasture but in an image of gracious suburban living which he created through advertising and public relations.

Our parents were taught to want a vine-covered cottage in a sylvan suburban setting. They were taught to enjoy commuting for hours in high-powered cars over four- and eight-lane freeways to get there. They were taught to believe that their children were underprivileged if they had to grow up in an urban environment. They were taught to cherish a life where everyone on their street was the same color, had the same income, the same aspirations, and lived in the same kind of house not over ten years old. Through the Federal Housing Act, the Federal Highway Act, the Federal Lending Act, our entire nation was led along the same rosy road toward suburban nirvana.

But we have awakened to the fact that neither satisfaction nor salvation is found in the suburbs. We can't run away from our problems or ourselves. In fact, maybe some of the answers to finding satisfying personal relationships, good housing, a sense of belonging, can be found back in the city, back in those old structures our forefathers built. And now it is our opportunity, and our responsibility, to dispel the previously taught negative impressions of urban living through using the same communications tools that the suburban developer used.

Wall murals have become a new tool in improving a neighborhood's identity. A neighborhood block party celebrates the creation of a "stage set" wall mural in background, sponsored by the Cambridge, Massachusetts Arts Council and designed by Jeff Oberdorfer. A mirror image of the neighborhood was painted on the blank expanse of an industrial wall. (Photo courtesy Al Gowan.)

Knowing Who We Are: The Inventory

The suburban developer not only did a successful job of convincing people that suburban living was attractive; but his communications campaign, and the subsequent negative impressions it fostered regarding the *déclassée* urban living, convinced both the remaining city residents and city decision-makers that the old urban communities were bad places in which to live.

It is the first communications responsibility of the preservationist to prove that his urban neighborhood indeed still has value, including architectural and historical value. Many urban residents feel that if their neighborhood has no value, if it is a slum, then they the people who reside there have no value either. Much of the crime, the vandalism, the graffiti is an expression by residents of frustration at being worthless, valueless, of having no positive identity of their own. Because of this pervading sense of despair, there is little chance of recruiting new residents or new pride into the community.

The one act which has started more urban neighborhoods on the road to recovery than probably any other is creating an inventory of historical and architecturally important structures of the area. The inventory offers credibility for the community. It officially certifies that, yes, this community indeed has structures which are historically important and architecturally important. At one time, famous and important people liked this area so much that they lived here. Celebrated architects built these buildings in a certain historic style with many interesting and unique architectural details.

During the actual process of the inventory, residents, professionals, hopefully the entire community and its outside decision-makers, are forced to actually look at the buildings and think about them. It is so easy to see only the debris, the superficial corruption of a community, without seeing the sturdy bones and flesh of the community itself.

The inventory is usually one of the first major undertakings after a neighborhood preservation organization is formed, following the catalytic crisis which was mentioned in the previous chapter. Old Town Restorations, Inc., Historic Savannah Foundation, Inc., the Historic Pullman

The inventory of historic architecture is the foundation for a community's revitalization process. The professional quality of the inventory and the publications which contain it can mean success for the restoring community.

Foundation, and many other successful preservation organizations each reacted to the initial crisis by asking themselves, "Who am I?" Through concerned residents working with qualified historians and architects, a block-by-block, house-by-house survey was made to define who built the structures, when, who lived in them, and what was their present quality of construction and maintenance.

The inventory is one of the most important first steps of communicating a new consciousness for the community. It is an opportunity for members of the community to become involved in a process of self-realization which goes far beyond just the physical drudgery of checking through dusty building permits at the Court House or walking rain-soaked streets assessing the condition of buildings. As one volunteer delightedly reported after days of searching through city directories and old newspapers, "Man, this neighborhood is something! All the important people lived here. The quality of life that went on here. Why, it makes me proud just to be part of it."

Once the inventory is accomplished and computated, the publication of the information is equally important. It can be the focus for your

future educational efforts. A good example of effective use of an inventory is the book *Building the Future from Our Past,* which was the final report of the St. Paul Historic Hill Planning Program published by neighborhood-based Old Town Restorations, Inc.

Old Town Restoration, Inc., through a planning grant from the National Endowment for the Arts and local foundations, created a comprehensive, interdisciplinary planning program for the community of which historical and architectural inventories were key elements. Using resident volunteers, students from the urban planning, architecture, and geography departments of local colleges, representatives from city agencies and historical societies, and other local architects and historians, a building-by-building survey was made of the entire six-square-mile area.

Following an initial "windshield survey" of the area, a comprehensive survey of 1,200 of the more architecturally important structures was made. Each building was rated between 0 (no value) and 3 (excellent value) under five separate architectural significance levels. In addition, historical, environmental, land use, as well as sociological studies, such as residents' age and economic status, were made. The 136-page book was published, discussed at neighborhood meetings, and presented to city agencies, financial institutions, and other decision-making groups. The book also contained an extensive list of Preservation Policies which were developed with the help of the St. Paul Planning Department and the Housing and Redevelopment Authority. This was the neighborhood "wish list" of community improvements the neighborhood associations took to the city for implementation.

Getting to Know Each Other: Neighborhood Meetings

No community event better illustrates Marshall McLuhan's treatise on social cause and effect, *The Medium Is the Message,* than the neighborhood meeting. Often the deteriorated community's problem lies in its own estrangement, both from itself and from others. Residents don't know each other or trust each other. The old battle cry, "United we stand, divided we fall," is as true today as it was in Revolutionary War times.

Developing an inventory can be a uniting factor, as can the publication and discussion of the results. When people get together, talk together about mutual concerns, insolvable problems become solvable. A new discovery is often made that the all-wise "they" who are supposed to have the power to make or break a community is a fiction. The real and only salvation is in the "we" of the community's united determination.

Meetings should take place frequently on many levels: general meetings for discussing the formation of a neighborhood organization, meetings to discuss the final report of the inventory, meetings for any major event in the life of the community. Committee meetings should also be held regularly to deal with the various elements of an over-all community preservation plan such as crime prevention, street improvements, development of new ordinances and developmental controls, park and open space improvements, traffic control, publicity, house tours, et cetera. Christmas parties, ethnic national holidays, and, of course, the annual house tour and preservation fair are all occasions for the community to communicate with itself and with others.

Welcoming the World: The House Tour

The nation is in the midst of becoming reacquainted with old urban neighborhoods. The one most effective welcome mat to the inner city has been the neighborhood house tour. Park Slope and Cobble Hill in Brooklyn, Fells Point in Baltimore, Marshall, Michigan, Historic Charleston, Milwaukee's Historic Walker's Point, as well as dozens of other communities, now have their own annual house tour which draws thousands of people to look and admire.

For many house-tour visitors, this may be the

Period costumes and a daylong celebration draw thousands of visitors to Galveston's restoring mixed-use community, the Strand. Sponsored by the Galveston Historical Foundation, Inc., "Dicken's Evening on the Strand" has become an annual event, helping to create a new image for the formerly neglected commercial street. (Photo courtesy Galveston Historical Foundation.)

first time they have ever dared to set foot in "the inner city." Many people call beforehand to see if it is safe to bring their children or drive their cars to the communities they have been educated to avoid. No amount of publicity can equal the personal, physical experience the suburbanite achieves when he walks the inner-city streets to discover that they are safe, to enter the restored old houses to discover that they contain luxuries of space and workmanhip his split-level rambler will never have, to talk with inner-city residents of all ages and colors, to experience the excitement of urban living.

Often in conjuncture with the house tours are various kinds of preservation fairs and historic events. Here residents can get together to exchange old-house-restoration ideas while newcomers learn a little about what makes an urban neighborhood work. In 1977, the annual Brooklyn Brownstone Fair drew a crowd of 15,000 to 20,000 people. Even a community as small as Marshall, Michigan, more than doubles its population the day the home tour and art fair begins.

The house tour fills a fourfold need: to unite residents in a common cause, to prove to them that other people see value in their community, to earn what can be a substantial amount of money for paying preservation organization expenses, and to welcome the world to a day in restored America.

Getting the Word Out: Community Publications

A monthly or at least quarterly newsletter is the voice of the community, helping new residents get to know the old-timers and helping city decision-makers to know they have an active new constituency to contend with. The editor of the newsletter has one of the most vital responsibilities in the community. It is up to the community to find that person and nurture his or her efforts.

A good editor can capture the personality of a neighborhood, urge a community's action on key issues, lay disturbing rumors to rest, inform public officials about the neighborhood's desires, and bring diverse community groups together. The newsletter should be a place for residents to ask

assistance, contribute knowledge, and express opinions. It can be as important a public service as city electricity and water to the growth and welfare of the community.

Neighborhood organizations should make financing of the newsletter its prime fund-raising responsibility. They should make sure that it is delivered to every resident as well as every local politician, banker, and other decision-maker in the city.

Getting to Know Your Local News Media

The city newspapers, radio and television stations shape public opinion as well as reflect it. How they handle a news item is as important as the news item itself.

Successful preservation communities have usually established close and mutually helpful relationships with their local news media. A restoring neighborhood can be tremendously newsworthy. This is not only due to the frequent clashes between residents and the Housing Authority or residents versus the city council or a developer. There are many positive and interesting stories that can make very good newspaper and broadcasting copy. For example: the spectacular transformation of an abandoned old wreck into a beautiful home, the excitement of a street fair or house tour, the drama of a young couple restoring their home by themselves, the unique history and architecture of the community—all can be very profitable news items for the media and the community.

As in every part of the preservation process, it pays to plan your approach to your local news representatives. How can you turn a typical neighborhood happening into a news event? Is a neighborhood couple going to have an open house to show neighbors their newly restored home? Have them dress in period costumes, or develop a poster showing the cost saving they made by doing the work themselves, or have the house's earlier residents be present to recount the way the community was "back then." And, of course, give the reporter a personal invitation with a suggestion as to the dramatic possibilities of the news story.

Posters, worthy of displaying on one's wall, have become dramatic expressions of a revitalized community. Besides their aesthetic value, their back sides often contain recruitment information about the community and the preservation organization.

Not every thing that happens in your community needs the news media's attention. Establish your credibility as a good PR person by choosing the events that have real human interest or hard-news potential. Soon you may be able to boast, as can Arthur Ziegler, that hardly a day goes by when there isn't an article in the Pittsburgh papers about local preservation activity. One local television station even ran a brief weekly program on Pittsburgh architecture which became the longest-running TV program in the city.

Preservation is news today. By working with your news media, you can make the change from negative impressions to positive impressions about your community, too.

The Professional Touch: Multimedia Presentations

The next best thing to an annual house tour is an exciting and informative multimedia show about your community. One of the important contributions to the revitalization of the Historic Hill District in St. Paul was a seventeen-minute slide show with recorded sound titled *The New Old Town in Town.* Created by members of the Ramsey Hill and Summit Hill neighborhood associations, it expressed in words and pictures just how beautiful restored houses can look and how delightful living in the Historic Hill could be. Over a two-year period, it was shown over one hundred times to every civic and social organization in the Twin Cities metro area, as well as to the officers of several banks, the chamber of commerce, and the city council.

This show was later replaced by a twenty-six-minute, three-screen slide show sponsored by Old Town Restoration, Inc., which dramatically expressed the success of the Historic Hill planning program and called for even more public involvement in the urban preservation process. This presentation has been shown an equal number of times to not only local groups but to organizations across the country.

Equally successful audiovisual presentations have been created in Pittsburgh, Baltimore, and many other cities. Again, it is the participation process which counts. If talented residents within the community can participate in the creation of the program, and if additional community resi-

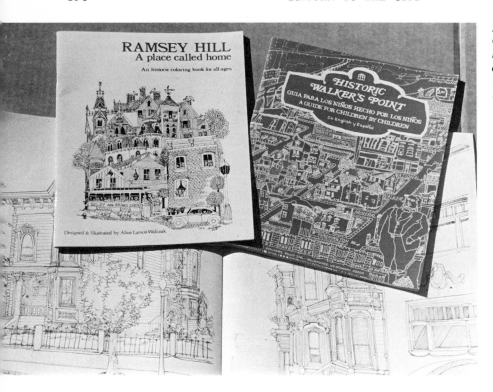

Don't forget the children. Coloring books, cutouts, booklets, often made by local children, are a good way to teach the preservation ethic early in life.

dents can participate in its presentation to local and state-wide groups, the entire community feels a part of the neighborhood's growing voice.

The Revitalized Neighborhood: A Creative Process

As was mentioned earlier, a special type of person is drawn to a restoring community. His or her attributes usually include imagination and creativity. Preservation is a creative process, and often a preservationist's sense of creativity expands beyond the limits of old-house restoration. A need to celebrate the restoration of old homes and communities by interpreting the process in an art medium can enhance the growth of a community as well as the creative growth of the artist.

This may be the reason why so many art fairs and craft fairs occur in restoring neighborhoods, especially during house-tour weekends. The preservation artists are pleased to be able to display their artistic creations as well as their restoration creativity to visitors. Whether the creation is a

The preservation artist uses every artistic medium to express his or her own personal passion for old houses and old neighborhoods. For example, Kevin O'Hare of Alameda, California, will sculpt your Victorian house, or he'll be happy to sell you one he has already made.

Alyce Walczak of St. Paul has helped many people to see old houses in a new perspective, thanks to her sketches. To entertain, to inform, to educate, the artist adds a significant force to the preservation movement.

pen-and-ink sketch, a mural on a wall, a sculpture, a painting, photography, original clothing designs, a multimedia show, or unique furniture or interior decoration, part of urban living is the freedom to express your best creative potential.

It is all part of creating a new identity for a restoring community, part of the process of un-slumming the image of a neighborhood and its occupants. Self-pride, self-expression are the enemies of the slum mentality. Creative expression is the light that chases away the darkness of ignorance and despair. Through effective communication and creative self-expression, fewer outside opinion-makers will be able to lay the destructive label of "slum" on a community or its residents. Old houses and old neighborhoods are too valuable, too rich in the good earth of history and humanity, to not allow the essential creativity of its environment to bloom like a garden. This makes everybody's world a little more beautiful, while restoring a community's pride as well as its past.

How to Assure Design Unity: In a Building, a Community

People are attracted to the urban environment because of its diversity. The human mind is challenged by the diversity of the people and ideas of the city. The human soul is stimulated by the aesthetic diversity of the city, its elaborate old structures that are a feast of different ages and styles and materials.

Yet, in spite of this architectural diversity, there is a unity, a rhythm, that is reassuring. In city neighborhoods, "home" is not just your own residence with the lock on the door. Home is the street, walled with eighteenth- and nineteenth-century façades of other homes, ceilinged by overhanging trees or the sense of enclosure created by the roof lines above, floored by cobblestones, bricks, or green grass. And your urban furnishings are the lampposts, shrubbery, iron fences, postal boxes, and, above all, the people who create the heartbeat of your urban environment.

In most old neighborhoods, in some miraculous way, this diversity all comes together in a living, human-scale unity. If you walk down the cobblestoned streets of Beacon Hill in Boston, or among the Victorians on Nob Hill in San Francisco, or on New Orleans' Bourbon Street, the streetscape embraces you. You feel comfortable there. You know where you are, on a street with a compatible, definite, whole identity. You are enclosed, surrounded, comforted and protected by the streetscape itself.

Why do many old urban neighborhoods give you these sensations? Probably because these neighborhoods were built before the sterile open spaces and high rises of the modern city planner's concept of the City Beautiful, before the disruption of eight-lane freeways and hundred-mile-per-hour automobiles, before the era of the franchised storefronts where every main street in America looks alike. Prior to 1900, few buildings could be constructed higher than four stories, streets were built for leisurely walking instead of high-speed through traffic, building materials were nature's own masonry and wood, and labor was inexpensive enough to allow time to carve and saw intricate decorations that delighted the eye.

Buildings were built by people, not mechanized assembly lines. Streets were built for people, not the internal combustion engine. The historic city was built for a community in all its diversity, to be used every hour of every day, every day of every year. The shopping center, the living and working centers were all one and the same, all within leisurely walking distance of each other.

In the past, builders seemed to have had more sensitivity to the surrounding structures. For example, in Charleston, where a street of buildings may range in age from one hundred to three hundred years old, each exists comfortably next to the other even though each may be of strikingly

When there are no use and design controls, almost anything can happen to old architecture, and it usually does. The results can be anything from misguided "improvements" (left) to new construction that is out of scale and character (right).

different architectural style. The unifying factors of the human-scale three or four stories, the use of brick and South Carolina pine, the eminently compatible style of the pre-Revolutionary, post-Revolutionary, Ante-Bellum, and even the "modern" of the 1860s up to the early 1900s, all flow in scale and architectural harmony. Even a modern service station on Market Street is of inconspicuous Colonial design to merge with the street.

Yet some architects and developers may scoff at such urban design "old-fashionedness" which does not use the more economically efficient "highest and best use" of land for steel-and-glass high-rises, plastic fast-food franchises, and the modern architect's passion for monolithic concrete creations. The preservationist may wish to remind the architectural modernists that like many successfully preserved cities, Charleston's economy is one of the healthiest in the nation, its community leaders still live downtown, and the typical old building is practically worth its weight in gold. Preservation still pays because the basic design unity of old streetscapes still provides the best quality of life and of business.

What Creates a Human-scale Streetscape?

Many of us need to be re-educated in the basics of what makes a community livable. We have for too long depended on the experts—the planners, the architects, the engineers, the developers—to tell us how to live. The results often have been the creation of an unlivable environment.

For example, a recent study prepared for the federal Law Enforcement Assistance Administration gives architects a share of the blame for increasing vandalism, burglaries, and muggings in today's huge apartment projects. Instead of utopias shared by people of all ages and life-styles, the architects have created a "no man's land" of crime and decay in the vast projects. Their major failure was in not providing "defensible space," the report concludes. Defensible space is where the physical environment is broken down into defined enclaves that can be readily controlled and maintained by the residents themselves. The compilers of the report may not have known it, but they were talking about the dynamics of the historic urban streetscape.

The modern concept of "defensible space" is in reality how the early builders constructed the classic human-scale urban space. They dealt with human relationships: a reasonable height and scale of a building which allowed a human being to not feel overpowered by its height, not to feel estranged from the activities of the street below when one is seated by the window of an upper floor. This allows a mother to watch her child play on the sidewalk below. It allows the person on the street to feel himself a part of the streetscape instead of being intimidated by its massiveness. It is easy to get to know the resident on the top of a three-story building. It is impossible to have any relationship at all with the person living on the thirtieth floor.

We can also think of the streetscape as a picture frame which focuses not only our eye, but our life. The rhythm of the spacing of buildings on the street creates an element of harmony in a neighborhood's architecture. The relationship of materials used to construct the buildings can add a distinctiveness to the neighborhood. Common materials such as brick, wood, stone, stucco can enhance the visual "feel" of the street.

The relationship of textures is also important. Whether the buildings are predominantly smooth, i.e., stucco; or rough, i.e., tooled jointed brick or rough-cut stone; or horizontally textured, i.e.,

The framing of a street

Without buildings, *the space has no boundary, no definition.*

With buildings, *an enclosed space is created. And with roofs and cornices, the space has a top which conforms to the human scale.*

Adding a rhythm *of compatible architectural details —porches and bays, steps and plantings—the street becomes a comfortable room that relates to the person.* (Courtesy *The Salem Handbook* by Historic Salem Inc.)

lap-wood siding, etc., the totality of the building façades gives the pedestrian a sense of continuity.

The same compatibility in relationships of

architectural details such as windows and arches, or roof shapes and chimneys, are important in the over-all compatibility of buildings on a street. And, colors of the buildings can create either a soothing, blending effect or a disturbing, uncomfortable feeling.

What Destroys a Human-scale Streetscape?

It is interesting that many terms relating to architecture are human terms. For example, we talk about a structure which destroys the rhythm and relationships of a street as an "unsympathetic structure." Or we talk about a building that is demolished in the middle of a streetfront as making the street look like a woman with a front tooth missing.

The reason is that it is absolutely impossible to remove a piece of architecture from the human environment, from the people who must live with it. Too often architectural decisions are made in the antiseptic offices of the banker or developer, or in the ivory tower of the planner or architect.

The people who must live with a piece of architecture are not only its builders and tenants, but also the people who must live near it or pass by it every day. These are the people who the architect and the builder must be sensitive to and sympathetic with. A garish, obtrusive building is a crime against the public.

It is long past the time when the private person can say "the public be damned." As long as the streets are public, the construction or removal of buildings on that street must be sensitive to both the surrounding architecture and the people.

Some Design Considerations

Today many preservation organizations, as well as some city planning departments, are creating design criteria to help preservationists restore old buildings and streets to a compatible sense of human scale and historic architectural relationships. These criteria also help the developer to create a new infill building which is sensitive to the scale and design of the structures surrounding

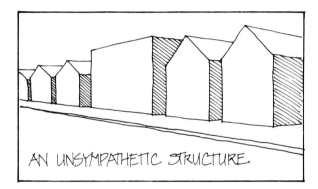

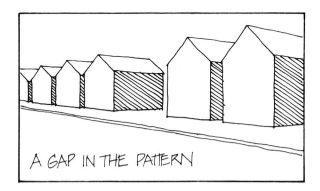

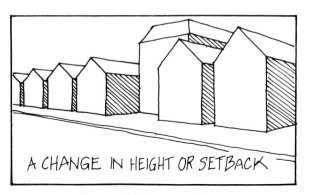

How to destroy the harmony of a streetscape
(Courtesy *The Salem Handbook* by Historic Salem Inc.)

it. (Also, see National Register check list, final chapter.)

Many developers and architects accuse preservationists of being antiprogress or wanting to keep cities pickled in the brine of eighteenth- or nineteenth-century architecture. This is not true. Most preservationists are primarily concerned with the sensitivity of the new development to its neighbors, not with new construction itself. Some architects and developers, the good ones, can create a modern building that is totally acceptable in most historic neighborhoods. These design guidelines should not hinder the architect. They should only challenge his creativity to provide the best possible product for his client and the community.

Each community should create its own criteria consistent with its own architecture. But much of the criteria can be used anywhere in America. For example, here is a list of fourteen criteria created by Old Town Restorations, Inc., for the Historic Hill District of St. Paul. Some of these items were taken from a previous preservation plan created for Savannah's historic district and were modified for St. Paul's architecture.

1. New structures or moved structures should be constructed at a distance not more than 5 per cent in front of the existing setback of adjacent buildings. New structures or moved structures can be constructed at a distance greater than 5 per cent from the existing setback of adjacent buildings only if the distance is behind the existing setbacks.

2. Building Height—New structures or moved structures should be constructed to a height within 10 per cent of the average height of existing adjacent buildings.

3. Proportion of a Building's Front Façade— The relationship of the height to width of new structures should be consistent with the ratio of the adjacent existing structures.

4. Proportion of Openings Within the Façade— The relationship of width to height of windows and doors should relate to the existing adjacent buildings.

5. Rhythm of Solids to Voids on Front Façade— The rhythm of structural mass to voids (openings) across the front façade should relate to rhythms established in adjacent buildings.

6. Rhythm of Buildings to Open Space Between —Passing down the street on any given block one experiences a rhythm of building masses to open spaces between them. This rhythm should be enforced where new construction or infill housing takes place.

7. Relationship of Materials—The structures within the State Historic District use several predominant materials: stone, brick, wood siding, and stucco. New structures should be constructed with the use of these materials.

8. Relationship of Texture—The predominant texture may be rough (stone, brick, stucco, wood shingles, tile) or smooth (vertical, horizontal, or diagonal wood siding). The exterior texture of new and rehabilitated structures should relate to and compliment these textures.

9. Relationship of Color—The use of color may be that of a natural material (red brick, yellow limestone) or a patina colored by time, or a painted surface. The color of new and rehabilitated structures (exterior, including the roof) should relate to and compliment the adjacent existing building.

10. Relationship of Architectural Details—Details may include cornices, lintels, arches, balustrades, chimneys, porches, bays, etc. New use or details in new structures should relate to the details of the existing adjacent area.

11. Relationship of Roof Shapes and Skyline— The majority of buildings in an adjacent area may have a gable, mansard, hip, or flat roof. The roof shape of a new structure should relate to the predominant roof shape of the existing adjacent buildings.

12. Scale—Scale is created by the size of units of construction and architectural detail which relate to massing of the structure as well as to human scale. Elements of scale may be brick or stone units, brackets and wood detailing on eaves, width of wood siding, window and door openings, porches and railings, et cetera. The scale of materials for new and rehabilitated structures should relate to the scale of existing adjacent structures. For example, narrow wood siding relates better to the massing of large structures than the commonly used wider aluminum horizontal siding.

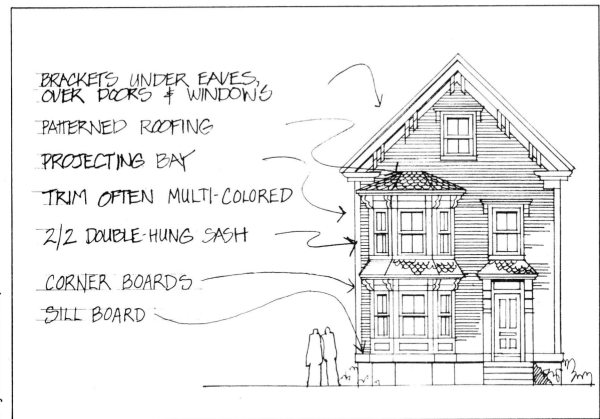

BRACKETS UNDER EAVES, OVER DOORS & WINDOWS

PATTERNED ROOFING

PROJECTING BAY

TRIM OFTEN MULTI-COLORED

2/2 DOUBLE-HUNG SASH

CORNER BOARDS

SILL BOARD

Appropriate restoration of a late-Victorian house

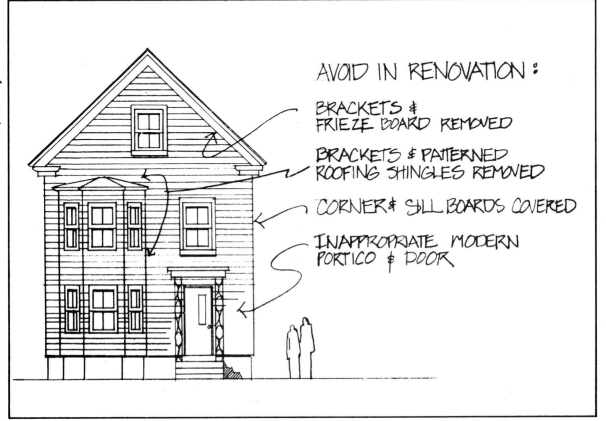

AVOID IN RENOVATION:

BRACKETS & FRIEZE BOARD REMOVED

BRACKETS & PATTERNED ROOFING SHINGLES REMOVED

CORNER & SILL BOARDS COVERED

INAPPROPRIATE MODERN PORTICO & DOOR

(Courtesy *The Salem Handbook* by Historic Salem Inc.)

Inappropriate restoration of a late-Victorian house

13. Relationship of Landscaping—There may be a predominance of a particular quality and quantity of landscaping. Any new structure should include landscaping as part of its construction plan.

14. Ground Cover—There may be a predominance in the use of brick pavers, cobblestones, granite blocks, patterned sidewalks, etc. A new structure should incorporate the use of existing ground-cover materials into its construction.

Of course, even these very general design guidelines will not please everyone. But they are at least a first step by a community which is trying to gain some control over its environment. Recently, there was a well-publicized dispute between Historic Hill preservationists and a new-building developer. Eventually, they arrived at a satisfactory compromise, thanks to the fact that the community had taken the trouble to create this list of design criteria.

Restoring Your Historic House

In this stage of American preservation consciousness, the demand to authentically restore the interior of an old building has become less acute. It is still preferable for a homeowner to as carefully as possible restore for historic authenticity, if possible, right down to the pull-chain toilet and kitchen fireplace or wood stove. But most of today's preservationists prefer at least a few modern amenities. Others prefer to use the interior space of an old building as a starting point for creation of an entirely new and modern living environment.

Most people feel that both types of old-house owners, the traditionalist and contemporist, can still be called preservationists if they at least carefully restore the exterior of the structure. While a modern transformation of the interior of a structure will please or offend only the guest who is invited inside, a radical change to the exterior will affect both the surrounding structures as well as the people walking by. Again, we are dealing with the concept of public sensitivity and compatibility. The streetscape is a public responsibility, a public trust to the community's identity.

More and more property owners are discovering that the authentic restoration of a building's exterior is not only good historic preservation, it is also good business. A co-ordinated streetscape of historical houses is a more attractive street, and each house is more valuable to the owner.

There is therefore more public support for publications such as *The Salem Handbook: A Renovation Guide for Homeowners*. Created by Historic Salem, Inc., it helps educate the homeowner to an appreciation of the history and architectural style of his home. It also provides basic information as to the do's and don'ts of historic restoration of his building's exterior. It is natural for most people to want to make their homes look beautiful. How-to books like this guide the homeowner on the pathway to a more sensitive kind of historic beauty, to authentic restoration and a greater resale value for his house.

Good historic design for old buildings is not some esoteric art. It is not antiprogress, or anti-business, or an elitist fad. It is just good common sense, an expression of neighborliness and community pride.

A restored building is aesthetically pleasing as well as economically profitable. Walking down a street lined with cared-for houses makes you feel good. Windows that match, buildings that complement each other, heights of structures that uplift instead of depress, textures of walls that harmonize, they all relate to the humanness in us. They make us alive and well. They make us part of the growing preservation movement whether we know it or not.

How to Gain Control
of Your Community

A deteriorating community is literally a place out of control. Like a vehicle racing downhill hell-bent for destruction, a slum has lost all control over its vital functions. External forces who come in with massive injections of money, usually only speed the sick community to an early death. It is only the community itself which can save itself by gathering together its lifeblood of buildings and people and attempting to create order out of a chaos of deterioration.

The creation of a neighborhood organization, as was outlined in the previous chapter, is the first step on a neighborhood's road to recovery. The second step is the neighborhood's inventory of historic and architecturally important structures. The third step is to learn how to exercise a community's muscles, to learn to function through self-control instead of living under the intensive care of external forces. As the purpose of the neighborhood survey was to ask the community question "Who am I?", the purpose of gaining control of one's environment is through asking the question "What do I wish to become?"

The neighborhood survey, if developed properly, should contain a list of goals and policies which evolve out of the process of identifying the physical and social assets and debits of the community. The implementation of these goals and policies, this community "wish list," can be the unifying force which will assure the continuing health of the neighborhood. What do you wish to accomplish? What needs to be done? Through these questions, you will soon discover that the basic problems of neighborhood deterioration, and the potential for solving those problems, lie in establishing controls over development, re-habilitation, and land use in your community.

Changing the Values of Urban America

We have trusted too deeply in representative government. Over the years, the earlier pioneering concept of participatory government turned to the concept of representative/caretaker government. We vote every two or four years, if we vote at all, in order to let someone else make the decisions for our welfare. This has often spawned a network of tax policies, zoning laws, and building codes which foster new development and speed the deterioration of the old. If we are to save our historic neighborhoods, we must participate in the establishment of new conservation values and new grass-roots legislation.

Historic zoning can be one of the most helpful and least expensive forms of preservation control for a community. An organization working to rehabilitate a neighborhood should first evaluate its city-zoning categories. The neighborhood may be zoned to allow uses inconsistent with its char-

A neighborhood out of control. Neglect, deterioration, abandonment, destruction can march down a street like an unchecked epidemic.

acter. For example, a residential area zoned to permit industrial, commercial, or high-rise development should be rezoned to reflect the existing residential character and to prevent incompatible development pressures. In some urban communities, mixed-use is the historic character of the area. In these, a controlled form of mixed-use may be acceptable.

Building codes can be some of the most insidious causes of a community's deterioration. Although they are created to maintain the health and safety of a neighborhood, they frequently cause the opposite. Building codes are designed by building and fire officials for modern structures and modern building methods to conform to stringent fire, health, and safety standards. The usual codes give no consideration to old buildings, other than to insist that old structures should somehow miraculously become new. The results are either that the codes are not enforced at all, allowing the structures to have no improvements, or the codes are fully enforced which forces the buildings to be torn down or radically reconstructed.

Some states and cities are changing their building codes, allowing alternative building regulations for the rehabilitation, preservation, restoration, or relocation of qualified historic buildings. The state of California has developed such a comprehensive new Historic Building Code. It authorizes the building department of every city or county to apply alternative building-code regulations to permit repairs, alterations, and additions to historic structures. The state also established a State Historical Buildings Code Advisory Board to assist in the implementation of the revised codes. It is important for preservation organizations to work with local building code officials, and the state legislature if need be, to create a building-code system which allows restoration of old buildings to be historically and economically feasible.

The surest way to protect an old building is to buy it. Another way is for your preservation organization to acquire an *easement* on a building's façade. For an agreed-upon price, the preservation organization purchases the assurance of the property owner that he will authentically

A neighborhood that does not demand zoning controls for compatible use, scale, setback, density, etc., can expect a deterioration of its character.

restore the façade of his building. This agreement is usually granted in perpetuity and accompanies the title to the land through successive ownerships. The property owner, meanwhile, continues to enjoy unimpaired control over the remainder of the property. Historic Annapolis, Inc., and the Pittsburgh History and Landmarks Foundation are two organizations which have used the façade easement as a preservation control tool. It is also a way to assist a poor homeowner to upgrade his property. The money supplied by the easement can be stipulated to be applied to restoration or maintenance of the property involved.

Other preservation organizations, such as the Greater Portland Landmarks, Inc., and Historic Savannah Foundation, Inc., use the control mechanism of *restrictive covenants*. When an organization purchases a historic property for resale, it can stipulate to the new owner that no alteration to the building's exterior can be made without the consent of the preservation group or its successors, that the group may sue the owner if he violates the agreement, and that the preservation group has the first option to repurchase the property if it is put up for sale. These contracts or covenants can run with the land, also.

The *transfer of development rights* is a preservation control concept which offers an effective bargaining tool if an important landmark is threatened with demolition because the owner feels the property is not profitable enough for him. For example, if a four-story historic building is on land zoned for a twenty-story high-rise, the landmark owner may sell the unused sixteen stories of development potential of his land to the developer of another site who wishes to create an even larger building beyond the zoning limits. The money gained in the transaction can be then used in the preservation of the landmark building. Of course, the transfer of development rights requires local legislative authorization and a sympathetic city council. New York City has tried to creatively use this newest form of preservation control with some success.

When all else fails, your organization may attempt to gain a *temporary moratorium* on all demolition within your historic district. This is one of the toughest political controls to achieve but if you are in the midst of a historic survey of the area, you may be able to secure at least a brief suspension of demolition permits by an understanding City Hall.

The Tax Reform Act of 1976

The best controls over demolition of historic properties, and the incentives to restore them, are still economic controls. Most destruction of old buildings is not caused by the fact that people dislike old buildings so much as the fact that our tax laws make it economically beneficial to tear them down.

Section 2124 of Public Law 94–455, the Tax Reform Act of 1976, is a major breakthrough in the attempt to both stimulate rehabilitation and to discourage destruction of historic buildings. It may become one of the best control tools that the preservationist has at his disposal.

Major tax incentives are provided for rehabilitation by owners of commercial or income-producing historic structures, which include residential rental properties. The act allows the owner of a "certified historic structure" to deduct for federal income tax purposes over a sixty-month period the costs of "certified rehabilitation," even if the expected life of the improvements exceeds sixty months, in lieu of otherwise allowable depreciation deductions. If the property qualifies as "substantially rehabilitated historic property," the owner may instead depreciate the basis or cost in the entire structure at a faster rate than the rate the owner otherwise would be allowed to use. In other words, where an owner was previously required to spread his tax deductions over the life of the property, now the deductions can be taken in five years.

Taxpayers will also be allowed to depreciate substantially rehabilitated historic property as though they were the original users of the property. The law defines substantially rehabilitated historic property as any certified historic structure with respect to which capital expenditures for any certified rehabilitation during the twenty-four-month period ending on the last day of any taxable year, reduced by depreciation or amor-

tization deductions, exceed the greater of the adjusted basis of the property or $5,000. The effect is that owners of certified historic structures will be encouraged to substantially rehabilitate their properties because they are allowed a more advantageous method of depreciation.

The Tax Act also encourages the charitable donations of historic property. Section 170(F)(3) of the code provides that a deduction is allowed for the contribution to a charitable organization (see why it pays to gain nonprofit status for your organization?) or a government entity exclusively for conservation purposes. Gifts can be for (1) a lease, or option to purchase, or easement with respect to real property of not less than thirty years duration, or (2) a remainder interest in the real property. Leases, options to purchase, or easements for real property donated after June 13, 1977, must be granted "in perpetuity." The law defines conservation purposes as the preservation of land areas for outdoor public recreation or education or scenic enjoyment, the preservation of historically important land areas or structures, or the preservation of natural environmental systems.

The Tax Act is equally clear on the negative tax consequences to the demolisher of a historic building. It provides that an owner or lessee of a "certified" historic structure cannot deduct any amounts expended for its demolition. Furthermore, the law provides that any building or other structure located in a Registered Historic District will be treated as a certified historic structure unless the Secretary of the Interior has certified, prior to the demolition of the structure, that it is not of historic significance to the district.

For tax purposes, demolition or losses sustained as a result of demolition must be added to the capital account as part of the cost of the land, rather than being deductible as part of the cost of the replacement structure. The effect of this provision is to discourage the demolition of certified historic structures because the taxpayers will not be able to deduct these costs.

Another part of Section 2124 (c) prohibits the accelerated method of depreciation for any property in whole or in part constructed, reconstructed, erected, or used (after December 31,

1975, and before January 1, 1981) on a site which was, on or after June 30, 1976, occupied by a certified historic structure which was demolished or substantially altered, other than by a certified rehabilitation.

The effect of this provision is to discourage the demolition of certified historic structures by limiting taxpayers to the straight-line method of depreciation, which provides less of a tax deduction in the early years of a project than does the accelerated method.

Historic Designation, the Key to Becoming a "Certified" Historic Structure

One of the most important reasons for the creation of a historic inventory for your community is to gather information needed to certify structures for historic designation. Almost any type of zoning, legislative, or tax control in historic preservation is contingent upon the property having some sort of certified historic designation. In other words, the structure must be authentically of historic or architectural importance in order to have preservation value.

Historic designation may come from certification as a Local Historic Structure or District, a State Historic designation, or being placed on the National Register of Historic Places. For the purposes of the Tax Act of 1976, a "certified historic structure" is either (1) listed individually in the National Register of Historic Places, or (2) located within and certified by the Secretary of the Interior as being of historic significance to a district listed in the National Register of Historic Places, or (3) located within a historic district designated under a state or local statute that has been certified by the Secretary of the Interior.

If your city does not have a Historic Designation statute, your preservation organization may wish to lobby for one. Criteria should include a statement of purpose to preserve and rehabilitate buildings of historic significance in your district. The statute must also provide for a duly designated review body, such as a review board or commission, with power to review proposed al-

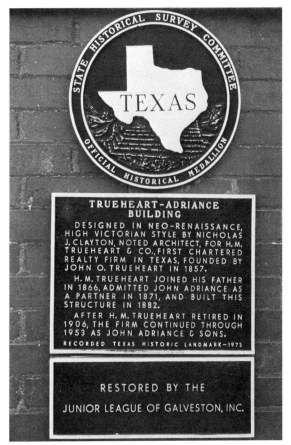

Historic designation for buildings and districts can be the most powerful tool the preservationist has. Designation gives value to the structure, encouraging organizations and individuals to invest in the community.

terations to structures within the designated district.

The National Historic Preservation Act of 1966 expanded the National Register of Historic Places from being only a register of National Historic Landmarks to provide broader preservation protection. Today, places of local, state, regional, or national significance in American history, architecture, archaeology, or culture can have the prestige and protection of a National Register designation.

Safeguards include not only the 1976 Tax Act benefits, but federal regulations also require that whenever historic property might be affected by a federally funded or licensed project, the head of the federal agency conducting the project must request an opinion from the Secretary of the Interior regarding the eligibility of the property. If the Secretary determines that the property is eligible for the National Register, then it must be afforded the same protection as property which has been officially nominated and placed on the Register.

The safeguards establish detailed procedures to determine the effect of the undertaking on the property. The regulations provide for Advisory Council review and comment before registered properties or their surroundings can be altered or demolished. These safeguards do not extend to private or state-supported projects.

In addition, listing on the National Register makes private property owners eligible to be considered for federal grants-in-aid for historic preservation through state funding programs.

How to Get Your District on the National Register

First, get to know your State Historic Preservation Officer (SHPO). The National Historic Preservation Act is implemented in co-operation with the SHPO, who is responsible for administering the National Register Program. Before properties are nominated for inclusion in the National Register, a statewide survey of historic, architectural, archaeological, and cultural resources is undertaken, of which your local survey could make a significant contribution. Before submission to the National Register, all nominations must have been approved by a State Review Board. If the property meets National Register criteria, the board recommends it for nomination to the National Register.

What chance does your neighborhood or your property have to achieve National Register designation? The selection process lies in the quality of significance in American history, architecture, archaeology, and culture which your district, site, or structure has, as well as its integrity of location, design, setting, materials, workmanship, feeling, and association. In addition, it depends on whether your district or structure:

1. Is associated with events that have made a significant contribution to the broad patterns of our history, or

2. Is associated with the lives of persons significant in our past, or

3. Embodies the distinctive characteristics of a type, period, or method of construction, or that represents the work of a master, or that possesses high artistic value, or that represents a significant and distinguishable entity whose components may lack individual distinction, or

4. Has yielded, or may be likely to yield, information important in prehistory or history.

But, even if your district or structure has been certified by your city, state, and nation, it is still not safe from misuse or demolition. Private property in America, as well as state, or city-owned property, can often be dealt with pretty much as the property owner sees fit. No historic structure is completely safe.

Only a basic change in public attitude toward more respect for historically and architecturally important structures will assure any degree of safety. Also, more public involvement is needed in the community decision-making process of community development, as well as more control through the establishment of advisory and regulatory bodies which were briefly mentioned before, such as:

1. Landmark commissions, or Cultural Heritage boards. These are local advisory boards created at the city or county level to designate or recommend designation of buildings as official landmarks. The ordinance creating these commissions often grants them the power to delay the demolition of buildings that have been so designated.

2. Historic District commissions, or Architectural Review boards. These are boards created to administer historic ordinances enacted by city and county governments. The commissions often have the power to establish architectural standards for alternations and new construction within the historic district. They can also have the power to prohibit the destruction or modifica-

tion of significant buildings within the districts.

3. And besides your neighborhood association, you may wish to establish a Private Historic Preservation Corporation. This can be a local or state-wide private nonprofit foundation which is incorporated to encourage preservation by performing educational functions to increase public awareness of preservation issues. Your organization may also take a more active role by purchasing or renovating historic structures for resale to persons willing to maintain them.

In conclusion, we may as well admit that there is no one way to control the deterioration and destruction of our historic America. Preservation is a process of education, legislation, and involvement in the democratic regulatory establishment. Thanks to a greater national awareness of the benefits of historic preservation, and the increased courage of local preservationists to get involved in the public arena of politics and economics, there are more and more ways for us to preserve and improve our environment.

How to Put New Life into Old Structures

In the seedy South End of Boston, next to the railroad tracks, stands an old brick two-story factory building. It can in no way be considered "historic," but it suggests how far the concept of preservation has come from the saving of George Washington's exquisitely beautiful and historic Mount Vernon.

Sullivan's Heating and Plumbing Company is still operating on the first floor of the building, but three people now live and work in the approximately 3,500 square feet of loft space on the second floor. Al Gowan, a designer, writer, and teacher at the nearby Massachusetts College of Art, Stephen Rose, antique photo dealer and teacher, and his wife Sara Blackburn, nutritionist and clothing designer, have transformed commercial space into home, workshop, and display rooms. An open loft has become fourteen rooms, two homes, a mutually satisfying living and working arrangement.

The enormous change in land use and life-style represented at the end of this Boston dead-end

Sullivan's Heating and Plumbing Company, a building of little historic merit. Yet it has great potential for economical loft living.

street indicates a revolutionary shift in American attitudes which is just beginning to be understood. Although many people still dream of a vine-covered cottage in the suburbs, a significant number of Americans are opting for a new kind of home in a factory loft, a Midwestern potato warehouse, or almost every kind of recycled commercial or institutional building imaginable.

The artifacts of the industrialization and mass production of America in the late 1800s have now become the resources for living environment and cottage industries in the 1970s. Economically, some modern pioneers are learning to support themselves by working and selling out of their home, bypassing employers and marketing middlemen. Emotionally, they are returning to the early American concept of the extended family where friends and relatives shared living spaces as well as living costs. In Boston, New York, Minneapolis, and Galveston, people living in recycled structures feel they have found the best way to return to the city.

Higher land values, interest rates, taxes, and soaring construction costs have doubled the price of new home construction in the last five years and multiplied it nine and a half times in the last fifty years. The size of the average new American apartment has shrunk 6 per cent in two years, from 996 square feet to 938 square feet. Ceilings are getting lower and rooms smaller. The alterna-tive to a shrinking living environment is the nation's old and often abandoned buildings. Restoring old homes for new living is the major part of historic preservation. But recycling other old buildings for new living as well as commercial spaces is a growing part of the preservation movement.

It's getting so you can't find a good industrial slum anymore, says Al Gowan. He expresses a growing complaint of the artists who were the first people to move into the dusty twelve- to twenty-foot-high industrial lofts in most inner cities. It takes a creative and courageous person to make a home from a cavernous space with no sinks, no toilets, no proper wiring, no heat, and often no sympathy from city authorities. Most industrial areas are zoned to prohibit residential use, so the earlier pioneers set up housekeeping like fugitives, making improvements to their apartments without building permits or official sanction.

Most building owners rented the debris-strewn spaces "as is" to people with little money looking for a large place in which to live and work. The average loft-liver did his own remodeling and improvements. But the price was unbeatable, often 2,000 square feet of space renting for as little as $75 to $200 a month. After installing plumbing, wiring, and heating, sanding and finishing the thick hardwood floors, painting walls and

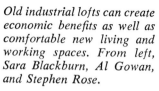

Old industrial lofts can create economic benefits as well as comfortable new living and working spaces. From left, Sara Blackburn, Al Gowan, and Stephen Rose.

Large open spaces with minimal divisions create working areas for Sara Blackburn's clothing designing studio and Stephen Rose's photography studio.

chemically cleaning the brick ones, the tenant may have spent from $2,000 to $5,000. If he can negotiate a long enough lease, the economic benefits of loft living are still very good.

But, today, the middle class and young professionals are discovering the aesthetic advantages of alternative living spaces. The huge rooms, large windows, natural brick walls and varnished wood floors, the twenty-four-hour urban atmosphere now command double or triple the rents first asked. The artists and craftspeople move on to less desirable neighborhoods, looking for the landlord who still hasn't discovered that his dingy warehouse may soon be the next recycled condominium or luxury apartment.

The developers have also discovered the advantages of recycled space. Even with complete, professional renovation of an old industrial building, a builder can still come out of the project often for half the cost of new construction. Only a few blocks away from Sullivan's Heating and Plumbing Company is the Boston waterfront, which has probably the nation's most spectacular complex of commercial and residential re-use anywhere.

The Long Wharf, a beautiful block of granite warehouses built in the 1830s, has now been transformed into the Custom House apartments. Strikingly designed duplex two-bedroom apartments, which utilize the timbered roof and stone with brick walls of the original structure, rent for $650 and up a month; yet the cost of conversion was about $25 per square foot. The building with its unique site on Boston's waterfront has created a long waiting list for its apartments.

Only a short walk away is Faneuil Hall where Samuel Adams once plotted revolution against Great Britain. Next to that historic symbol is one of the greatest symbols of historic recycling of all, the $40-million restoration of 150-year-old Quincy Market's three block-long marketplace buildings. A normal city, full of restaurants, shops, and office space, is now crammed into these three buildings, drawing crowds that make every day seem like Christmas and Fire Sale Day all bundled into one.

The astonishing success of these waterfront recycling projects is finally beginning to educate bankers and developers to the fact that adaptive re-use of existing buildings makes more sense than building new from the ground up. In 1976, the value of building permits issued for all forms of alteration in Boston totaled $154 million. This is compared with only $41 million for new construction, which is a complete reversal from 1971, when new construction accounted for $454 million or 90 per cent of total permits, and when many people wanted to demolish the entire waterfront. Today, developers are making plans for almost every building in sight, including the Suffolk County jail which was condemned as unfit for prisoners.

The Challenge of Using Existing Space

The concept of adaptive re-use has been the most dramatic force which has expanded historic restoration to the larger social and economic arena of urban preservation. The creative use of existing space, the combining of an innate need to remember our past with a world-wide ecological imperative to recycle our man-made resources, has opened a whole new series of solutions to national problems.

Old buildings may not only be historic; they are also usually incomparably well and strongly built. They were constructed before the modern architect was forced to compromise with impossible labor and materials costs which demanded an elimination of so-called superfluous space, materials, aesthetics, and craftsmanship.

Historic old buildings, beautiful old buildings, like Quincy Market in Boston or the Stewart Title Building in Galveston or San Francisco's City of Paris Building, have re-use potential even a blind man can see. But the uncounted numbers of old but still serviceable buildings in our nation's cities and countrysides, which do not have the distinction of stained glass or marble halls yet still offer new uses, are the real challenge for the preservationist.

Garages and livery stables seem especially amenable to adaptive re-use because of their high ceilings and expansive open spaces. In Marshall, Michigan, where people have an unusual appreciation for old structures, one of its most impressive adaptive re-use projects is the transformation of an 1857 livery stable and garage into the city's Town Hall. It is symbolic of the imagination of one of the town's greatest preservationists, Harold Brooks, and the general attitude of the entire community.

Victoria Crossing was simply a 1920s structure of two-story brick storefronts and an old garage on the corner of Grand and Victoria in St. Paul.

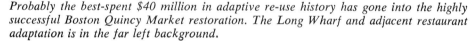

Probably the best-spent $40 million in adaptive re-use history has gone into the highly successful Boston Quincy Market restoration. The Long Wharf and adjacent restaurant adaptation is in the far left background.

But because of the imagination of its young developer James Wengler, it has now become a handsome, modern, miniature shopping mall. An interior court and circulation sidewalk has been created with brick paving and shrubbery. A huge skylight over what was the garage has created an ideal climate for shopping and sociability even in the coldest Minnesota winter.

The recycling of the Victoria Crossing Mall has sparked other re-use ventures on the street. An old automobile dealership has become the attractive headquarters for the Minnesota Opera. Across the street from that was a used-car lot. It is now being replaced by a new structure containing one hundred luxury condominiums and a parking ramp, thanks to the surrounding adaptive re-use projects which are increasing the economic confidence of the community. An exciting

Stewart Title, a national title company, invested $300,000 in the exterior restoration and interior renovation of this 1882 building on Galveston's The Strand.

A reception area in the renovated Stewart Building, facing the main interior hallway.

What was an old livery stable and garage has become an attractive landmark and Town Hall/Police Department for Marshall, Michigan. The essential quality of the structure along with re-use imagination made the difference. (Before and after photos courtesy the Marshall Historical Society.)

hub of neighborhood activity has been created through the discovery that not just historic preservation pays, but also that conservation and re-use of less than historic structures can provide dividends for private developers and for the entire community.

But how far can we go with the concept of preservation and adaptive re-use? Can we take it to the countryside, to structures with little historic and architectural merit?

On a rolling hillside near the rural community of Wautoma, Wisconsin, Ernie Reed and his wife, Gladys, created what may be the ultimate in adaptive re-use. They transformed a potato warehouse and grain-storage shed into a snug and modern retirement home.

The stone foundation of the warehouse, laid by Mrs. Reed's father around the turn of the century, is over three feet thick. The siding is of sturdy white oak and pine, sawed from local trees. After shopping for a ready-made house, they decided that economics and comfort dictated that their imagination and Yankee ingenuity would have to serve them. So, without the counsel of architect or accountant, they reconstructed the old farm building into a new home, complete with picture window.

Is this Wisconsin couple members of the traditional preservationist fraternity, or a country version of the urban adaptive re-use builder, or just two more Americans who have decided to trust to their instincts in appreciation of old buildings and making do with what they have? The challenge to creatively use existing space is

everywhere, from the Wisconsin farmlands to the Boston waterfront. The preservationist has become populist, a pragmatist who uses his past to build for the future.

How to Recycle, Re-use, Restore

Adaptive re-use is usually not as simple as restoring a home. If you are adapting a commercial space for residential use or an industrial structure for a different kind of commercial use, a thorough investigation of local zoning and building codes should be made. Many city codes prohibit alternative uses for commercial or institutional structures. Other codes may demand a drastic change in electrical, plumbing, and other services. Exits, stairways, room capacities, safety features may have to be drastically changed. For example, in some states, seismic-safety codes may require major structural strengthening of public buildings if use is to be changed. A preservationist may literally have to construct a new building within the old structure.

Therefore, know what to expect before committing yourself to what could be an overwhelming financial investment. If your local zoning and building codes seem unreasonable, try to work with local officials to change codes to allow more economically feasible adaptive re-use. Contact other cities for copies of their codes to prove to your local officials that public safety and recycling of old buildings can be compatible.

New York City has developed very progressive

What was an old potato warehouse and grain storage shed is now a comfortable retirement home. Ernie and Gladys Reed created the transformation without realizing that they also are in the great tradition of preservation and adaptive re-use.

code changes for loft conversions. Portland, Oregon, and Savannah, Georgia, have worked to solve code problems in multiple uses for commercial buildings. Sacramento and San Diego, California, are working to solve seismic-safety-code problems regarding re-use of old commercial buildings. Hard-liners in building and zoning departments around the nation are slowly beginning to soften regarding re-use projects.

Next, approach adaptive re-use in a practical, businesslike manner. Don't let your emotions outrace your reason when considering recycling an old building for a brand-new use. Do some marketing research first. Is there a need for the new use in this particular neighborhood? Is there sufficient customer traffic or demand? Will there be enough parking, related services, long-term consumer interest? How far can you reasonably expect the neighborhood to progress in six months, six years? Will the use you put to your building be compatible with the changing nature of the community? What safeguards can you reasonably expect to create in order to help protect your investment and improve the neighborhood? How much of a loss in money and time can you afford to take as you develop a market for your building's new use? Many of the questions which need asking are found in the Ideal Loan Application (see Economics chapter).

Financing is usually the critical step on the way to a successful adaptive re-use project. Many financial institutions are becoming more receptive to re-use projects *if* you can make a strong economic case for it on your loan application. Even in comparison to new construction, recycling makes good economic sense for the developer, the lender, and the community. Here is a typical economic comparison provided by restoration economist Richard Crissman:

	Deteriorated Commercial Building "as is"	Vacant Lot	New Office Building	Deteriorated Building Preserved and Recycled
Market value	$300,000	$350,000	$3,900,000	$800,000
Assessed value	75,000	65,000	975,000	200,000
Taxes	900	780	11,700	2,400
Jobs	3	1½	330	87
Average rent per square foot per month	5¢	N/A	3.80	2.52
Gross annual rent roll	2,400	3,900	684,000	126,000
Owner's net income	1,200	3,900	400,000	85,000
Net return on capital	0.4%	0.85%	10.25%	10.5%

But even if your persuasiveness cannot gain a loan, don't give up. Many shoestring developers have still been successful through a combination of their own investment of sweat equity and their tenant's. For example, Henry Willette used his own savings to purchase his first buildings in the Old Port Exchange district of Portland, Maine. He did much of the basic restoration work himself and rented space for low cost to tenants who agreed to renovate their own space. Through mutual self-help, the owner and tenant can restore a property between them.

Before beginning to rehabilitate a building, if is has any special architectural character at all, know what you are doing. More promising adaptive re-use projects have become failures because the owner attempts misguided improvements which detract from the structure's essential historical and architectural qualities. Turning a Federal style into "phony Colonial" or jazzing up a Queen Anne style with eighteenth-century-style brass door lamps will not attract the tenants or customers who appreciate old architecture. If you do not understand the values of design and

The re-use of old industrial buildings provides an opportunity for imaginative architecture. This exciting use of skylight and balconies has re-created a Galveston warehouse into modern luxury condominiums.

architecture, ask the assistance of someone who does. And just because someone did some nice things with red plush for your aunt Emma's boudoir does not mean that person is an expert in authentic Renaissance Revival architecture or can suggest compatible contemporary modifications.

If you do not plan to do much of the work yourself, or at least personally supervise it, one of the most important choices you can make is in your contractor or construction manager. Unfortunately, most contractors, carpenters, plumbers, et cetera, do not understand how to sensitively and efficiently restore or rehabilitate an old building. It takes a contractor with a great deal of experience, patience, and skill to solve the continuous problems that constantly arise in a renovation project. There is no standard operating procedure in restoring an old structure. Behind every wall and under every floor can be innumerable costly surprises. That is why few knowledgeable contractors will give you a firm bid on a restoration job, unless the building is to be completely gutted and a new interior constructed. Even this can pose surprises if the

building reveals hidden major structural defects.

Recycling and restoring old buildings are not easy tasks. Don't be lulled into thinking that every recycling project is simple, or profitable. Many of the successful developers learned their lessons through a couple of very unprofitable projects before they gained the wisdom and experience to create an adaptive re-use project that is both aesthetically and economically pleasing.

Ask any preservationist how many hours he had to spend in the offices of the city housing inspector and the planning commission. Ask him about the dozens of loan applications he made to dozens of financial institutions. Ask him about the painful days of attempting to work with a contractor who didn't know a modillion from a mullion.

But in spite of all the uncertainties and trials of adaptive re-use, most preservationists will also admit that it's all worth the creation of something new and useful out of a neglected old building. Putting new life in old structures is more than just an investment. It is a creative experience that is more fun, and often more rewarding, than building new from the ground up.

PART FOUR

Must Preservation Mean Displacement?

More people are displaced by neglect and deterioration of housing than all the back-to-the-city movements put together. Yet an ironic indication of the growing success of urban preservation is the accusation by some that the preservationist is a major cause of displacement of the poor. The assumption seems to be that if preservation would cease on old, often abandoned structures, then the problems of the poor would cease.

The new national consciousness of conserving and re-using old structures and old neighborhoods is one of the most significant changes of American attitudes since the Civil War. This growing public acknowledgment that our physical past has value and that our resources should be conserved can be equally freeing and uplifting to the cities' poor as it can be for the majority population.

As has been repeated throughout this book, preservation is a process, a tool for change in a community which can go well beyond the mere restoration of buildings for the white middle class. As with any dynamic process, it can get out of control, displacing not only the poor resident but the preservationist who restored the buildings in the first place. Yet this same process can also be the catalyst to create a well-balanced diversity of age, income, and race in the urban environment which existed during the late golden age of the cities.

A healthy economy is a mixed economy. A healthy community is a mixed community. The reason why many people are returning to the city is because of the deadly dull sameness of many white, middle-class suburban ghettos. Across the nation, in almost every restoring urban neighborhood, the reasons often given by people who have moved back to the city were, "The diversity . . . the different people and experiences . . . the chance for me and my children to live with people who have different backgrounds and ideas."

Of course, the one dynamic which always tends to eliminate diversity of income in a community is property values. A piece of property no one wants is valueless. So, rents can be afforded by even the poorest citizens. Yet if the same piece of property becomes coveted by everyone, it can have extraordinary value. Its price and rents rise accordingly, to force the poor tenant to find another less attractive home in a still unwanted part of the city.

If only this unrestrained fluctation of property values ruled the arena of urban restoration, then hope for the poor would be very bleak indeed. Then the sad pronouncements that the suburbs will be the next slums while inner cities become bastions of the rich could be true. But, fortunately, in many restoring communities, preservationists are as concerned about people as they are about architecture. In fact, they often are accomplishing significant social action by not

The need to preserve old buildings and old neighborhoods crosses all boundaries of race, interest, and income. Inner-city need not be a bad word if everyone works to make it a true "community" of people.

only improving the community through their own restoration projects but are also actively engaged in developing low-income housing programs in co-operation with local and federal agencies.

Creative new approaches are being taken to help people with little money to remain in their restoring communities. New ways are being found to help them also participate in the rewards of rehabilitated structures and revitalized, better-balanced neighborhoods of people.

"They ain't chasing me out. No sir!"

Pride in old buildings is not limited to the young, white college graduate. Of course, many of the urban poor would be just as happy to flee the neglected city for the suburbs as were their middle-class predecessors. Yet some of the poor can see past the deterioration of their homes and streets to appreciate their greater value of style and quality.

Mr. Bullet lives with his family of twelve children in a well cared-for Second Empire Revival-style house in Pittsburgh's Manchester neighbor-

hood. Across the street is a relatively new row of government-built low-rent houses. Next to him is an abandoned sister house to his which has been set afire five times in recent months.

He says that the children in the nearby housing project can't seem to stand the old houses like his. They burn them and take axes to their intricately carved front porches. He asked them why they bother the old houses, why they bother him as he sits on his front porch. The children reply that they don't have any front porches on their houses.

The vandalism may result from sheer boredom. But he reflects that they also may be a little jealous of the old houses with all the funny, fancy woodwork and pretty glass windows. His home is a real home, he says. It feels like home, not like some motel where you can't feel right to unpack your bags. He proudly displays the white marble fireplace in his front room and fondles the carved-oak banister. He has lived here for fifteen years. Nobody can chase him out. No sir, this here is home.

Old houses give some people a sense of identity, a sense of pride, that cannot be replaced

Mr. Bullet of Pittsburgh is proud of his house. New houses just don't have the good feelings and good spaces that an old house has. He's going to stay here, no matter what.

in a shiny new house. These people have a right and a responsibility to remain in their communities, to be restored by the neighborhood as it is restored. Fortunately, many people who are newly discovering the old, forgotten neighborhoods understand this importance, not only for the welfare of the old residents but for the new residents as well.

One of the most articulate and successful advocates of stay-in-the-city preservation is Arthur Ziegler, Jr. He is helping long-time residents like Mr. Bullet to remain. He, through the Pittsburgh History and Landmarks Foundation and in cooperation with the city, is finding creative preservation solutions to the problems of deteriorated buildings and the displacement of the poor. The

Pittsburgh Urban Redevelopment Authority, instead of tearing down buildings in the badly deteriorated Manchester district, is now buying the rights from the homeowner to restore the building's façade and is offering 3 per cent HUD 312 Rehabilitation Loans or giving outright grants to people who can't even afford the 3 per cent loans. In addition, the city offers free rehabilitation specifications and free construction supervision for the poor preservationist.

In the Mexican War Streets district, the Landmarks Foundation created the first preservation effort in the nation which provided housing for low, moderate, and middle-income people.

For the poorest residents, the Foundation utilized the Leased Housing Program of the federal government. They bought derelict houses, restored them fully, and then rented them at slightly below market rates to the housing authority. The authority then sublet the houses to low-income families at even lower rents and also performed routine maintenance on the dwellings. The tenants' initial five-year leases, signed before work began, enabled the Foundation to obtain mortgage funds.

For moderate-income residents, the Foundation purchased deteriorated houses and rehabilitated the most obvious deficiencies such as electrical systems and shabby interiors. By keeping costs down as well as causing minimal disruption to the house, they were able to retain the low rents and the same tenants.

In order to bring young middle-income residents into the neighborhood, the Foundation purchased some of the most deteriorated housing, assembled their own restoration crew, and restored the structures. Pleasant apartments were created within the restored exteriors, retaining as much of the old mantles, woodwork, and hardware as possible.

In these ways, Ziegler and the Foundation were able to balance the equation for long-term preservation success; restoration of structures for the retention of both the present low-income residents and the attraction of a stabilizing middle-income population. By controlling, and reducing, the costs of restoration, the land values were held to a level that did not force low-income people out of the community. Similar projects are happening in Savannah and other cities, where preservation corporations are doing nonprofit rehabilitation to insure that rents and property values will be reasonably controlled.

Getting a Piece of the Action

The renter is usually at a disadvantage in a restoring community because he has no direct control over the escalating value of the property in which he lives. If he is not fortunate enough to live in a building controlled by an enlightened preservation group such as Ziegler's, the open-market value of the house and its rents could rise drastically.

A homeowner, on the other hand, has more control over the property in which he lives, although even he must contend with rising taxes and repair costs. But at least, if property values rise in his community, the increased values can work to his advantage instead of disadvantage. In addition, the homeowner, because he feels more in control of his home and his neighborhood, can often be expected to maintain his house better and be more concerned with community improvement.

Therefore it is no wonder that many of the urban poor are working to own their own homes and reap whatever benefits come from physical and social improvements in their community. Because of this, the concept of urban homesteading is offering the greatest promise for long-term solutions to both the problems of displacement and of deterioration.

Baltimore, Maryland, has one of the nation's largest urban homesteading programs. Through the HUD Section 810 Urban Homestead Demonstration Program, low-income residents receive special assistance in acquiring and rehabilitating abandoned houses. Households with a median income of only $8,826 have become homeowners through this federally guaranteed program.

As was mentioned earlier in this book, another very dramatic homesteading concept is happening in New York City. The Urban Homesteading Assistance Board, sponsored by the Cathedral of St. John the Divine, assisted in the rehabilitation of over 1,000 units of housing by 1977, creating decent and low-cost homes for families in Harlem, the Lower East Side, the South Bronx, and other low-income neighborhoods.

Their concept of sweat-equity homesteading, utilizing the personal rehabilitation of abandoned multiple dwellings, is the lowest-cost method of re-creating good housing anywhere. The total development cost for a two-bedroom apartment averages $15,000. This compares with a per unit development cost of around $32,000 for gut rehabilitation by conventional contractors and about $45,000 per unit for new construction.

Typical monthly carrying charges for a sweat equity homesteading two-bedroom apartment range from $150 to $180. This contrasts dramatically with the subsidized-rent level of $491 per month permitted for rehabilitated apartments under the federal government's Section 8 rent-subsidy program. Because UHAB's sweat-equity program usually helps tenants form a co-op ownership arrangement of their buildings, the tenant is in fact part owner of the structure, giving him both the security and pride of home ownership.

UHAB homesteaders also may receive additional assistance through a federal job training program which pays a training stipend to construction trainees. Unemployed homesteaders can, therefore, learn valuable job skills while they rehabilitate their homes. Through the middle-class ideal of home ownership and his special job skills, the homesteader may finally be able to rid himself of the damning title of "the poor." As many people declared during the depression of the 1930s, "I may not have any money, but I'm not poor." The difference is a sense of pride, a sense of place.

Freedom to Rent Helps Prevent Displacement

It is easy for the poor person to feel trapped. When his community is taking that long slide into deterioration, he can't afford to move away. And when the community is restoring itself and things are improving, then he often can't afford to stay. This is especially true for the renter, who

Baltimore has one of the most active urban homesteading programs in the nation. Hundreds of abandoned homes are now being restored, like the house on the left, to help new owners stay in the city as well as return to the city.

must ride the waves of rising "market rate" rent charges as best he can with what little income he has.

Previously, the federal government tried to help improve the living conditions of the poor through building special "public housing" units. But these massive and expensive projects were often more destructive to the occupants than the slums they left. For example, Pruitt-Igoe was a St. Louis Housing project, consisting of thirty-three, eleven-story buildings with almost 2,800 apartments. Within five years it became a national scandal of crime, deterioration, and vandalism. Its dehumanizing, institutional appearance, and its eventual demolition, has become a symbol of the worst aspects of separation and institutionalizing of the poor.

Today, one of the most promising experiments in assuring decent housing for the poor is the Department of Housing and Urban Development's Section 8 rent-subsidy program. The program, established by the Housing and Community Development Act of 1974, aids poor to moderate-income families whose income does not exceed a figure that is 80 per cent of the median income in their communities. It permits them to select their own apartments with the government assisting in the paying of the rent.

In theory, the program could be a good solution to a basic problem. It helps families live in quarters of their own choice rather than in public projects for the poor. In addition, the poor, with the assistance from the government, become a part of the "market demand force" which can stimulate landlords to improve their properties and developers to provide new housing as needed.

But there are problems, such as too much paperwork required by each applicant, often too low rent limits, a lack of apartments that are sound enough to meet HUD standards, and too much complexity in the program that tends to discourage tenant and landlord alike. Yet the essential concept of freedom of choice in housing for the poor is good. With more realistic rental levels and simplified procedures, both poor people and depressed neighborhoods could benefit.

HUD also has a program of home-ownership assistance for lower-income families which can be used in conjunction with other local home ownership programs. Called the Section 235 Home Ownership Subsidy Program, it provides assistance in the form of monthly payments to the property mortgagee, reducing interest cost to as low as 5 per cent. This is applied if the homeowner cannot afford the total mortgage payment with 20 per cent of his adjusted income.

The Savannah Landmark Rehabilitation Project, Inc., purchases deteriorated rental properties, rehabilitates them with the help of local residents who are paid through federal CETA on-the-job funding, and rents the property back at below-market rates to the original tenants. (Photo courtesy Savannah Landmark Rehabilitation Project, Inc.)

The Renegades of Harlem are working their way out of a ghetto existence by rehabilitating and gaining ownership of their co-op apartment buildings. Preservation has helped them learn a trade and become property owners.

As the urban preservation and adaptive re-use movements gain strength, the federal and local governments should be expected to respond. Imaginative new ways to help the poor stay in the city as well as concepts to help more middle-income people return to the city should evolve. Thanks to the several breakthroughs by preservation groups in discovering new solutions to the old problems of poor housing and poor people, this federal involvement should accelerate.

The challenge for a new urban "Marshall Plan" is clear. There are over five million structures in American cities that are in need of rehabilitation. There are millions of able-bodied people who need work. There are hundreds of thousands of families who need sturdy, safe housing. Our deteriorated urban communities are literally a gold mine of housing and of work for our nation's unemployed.

In New York City, Baltimore, Philadelphia, Cincinnati, Savannah, the poor are proving that they can be just as good preservationists as is the middle-income person. There is no more rewarding investment than to invest one's sweat in the restoration of an old building. A person is no longer poor when he has his own home and his pride.

Looking Beyond Preservation

The era of the suburb is over. The era of the split-level, 3,000-square-foot house on a one-acre lot, the typical large family with a full-time housewife, the three-car garage containing an assortment of high-powered cars and recreational vehicles, the entire glittering American banquet table of materialistic conspicuous consumption is coming to an end.

The era of the city has returned. Smaller is more beautiful. Older is more respectable. Recycling is no longer only what breweries do with used beer cans. In the last decade a profound change has settled over America. Our national birth rate has been cut in half, leaving smaller families and less need for big houses and suburban schools. More people are getting married later in life or not at all. Our divorce rate has increased drastically, creating more one- or two-member households. The fact of the critical shortage of traditional forms of energy is finally sinking into the consciousness of the homeowner and commuter. And the knowledge that crime is as common in the country as it is in the city has shown there is no escape from our national social problems anywhere.

In 1971, the median price of a new single-family home in this country was $25,200. In 1976, the median price was $43,100. In 1977, only one year later, it rose to $49,000. In some parts of the Southwest, the 1977 median price was $75,000 or more. The old American dream of a new home, a suburban home, is dying for almost everyone.

Part of the reason for the growing lack of livability of the suburbs is their lack of planning. New subdivisions grow like Topsy at the whim of a developer. Schools, water systems, sewage systems play catch-up in a costly scramble to reach the hop-skip-and-jump proliferation of housing tracts.

In newer cities, poor planning and the frantic pace of freeway building have created communities and entire metropolitan areas which are nothing more than transportation systems with attached bedrooms. Los Angeles, for example, utilizes 75 per cent of its land mass for the automobile. Houston, the nation's fifth largest city and called "the golden buckle of the Sunbelt," is beginning a slow slide from boom to bust. It has become a tarnished, congested, polluted replica of what is growing increasingly wrong with our suburbs and what had caused the decay of our older cities—the inability to plan ahead and weigh the costs of progress.

Today, as we see new hope for the restoring of our older cities, it is important that we look beyond the initial successes of urban preservation. How can we plan ahead, how can we protect our revitalizing community from becoming what critic Andrew Kipkind called "the new kitsch of ad-

Six Portland, Oregon, families found an innovative solution to a problem of restoring a row of six town-houses. By condominiumizing the property, each has their own home while developing the back yards as a common recreational area.

vanced capitalism." The few people genuinely concerned about history and architecture are struggling to save the few significant old buildings. Artists and craftspeople work to create a new life in old loft spaces. A broader range of preservationists and the poor attempt to build a healthy and diverse community out of the ruins of the past.

Then comes the deluge of chichi botiques, speculators to turn middle-class houses into high-priced condominiums, and the final transformation of what was a promising restoration of a well-balanced urban neighborhood turns into a commercialized caricature of an "Olde Towne" supermall.

How to Stop the Boom-and-Bust Cycle

Almost every process, from a students' grading system to the evolution of a community, seems to follow a bell-shaped curve. The low point, the gradually rising line to a high point, and then the slow downward trend to another low seem to be a universal graph of life's processes.

Our old inner cities have reached the low point. Now, thanks to the restoration of old structures and the growing return-to-the-city and stay-in-the-city movements, the curve is beginning to rise. In some communities such as Boston and St. Paul and Savannah, there is practically a boom of preservation activity. But how can we sustain this peak experience of a city's bell-shaped curve, how can we sustain the delicate balance of restoration and adaptive re-use enthusiasm along with the economic and racial balance of the community?

As was explained in the chapter on Economic Feasibility, there are four definite stages in the preservation process, from Abandonment to Respectability. But there can also be a Stage Five, Deterioration. Examples of the last stage are in portions of the Wells Street "Old Town" in Chicago and to some degree in the Gaslight Square area of St. Louis, where too-intense commercial activity and unsympathetic uses have harmed the growing public appreciation of the historic area.

Many people, preservationists and older residents alike, often wish that the urban preservation process could stop at the Stage Three Restoration phase where prices are still low, there is a fierce sense of community pride, and the speculators have not yet arrived. The Stage Four Respectability phase with its higher property values and more intense commercial activities can be the forewarning of Stage Five if care is not taken.

Even the enthusiastic politician and the moneyed developer should not equate faster rehabilitation activity and the fast turnover of original residents and preservationists with the long-term success of a community. The preservation process can be too fast and too successful. Enthusiasts

Authentic historic conversation in toto, preserving an entire neighborhood such as Boston's Charles Street area on Beacon Hill, can be more satisfying than tearing down the old and building new.

Stage Five of the preservation curve is reached when the restoration of a historic community again dips toward deterioration. Inappropriate uses, obtrusive signs, the discouragement of diversity in a neighborhood can spell trouble for even the best of old architecture.

for exposed brick, nostalgic restaurants, and candle shops can end up with a community which looks exactly like many other too-restored communities, as if McDonald's had decided to go into the preservation business.

Whatever the preservation efforts are in a community, its authentic identity should shine through. When you are in Quincy Market or the Old Port Exchange, you should know that you're not in Underground Atlanta or Denver's Larimer Square. Ramsey Hill in St. Paul should not end up looking like Society Hill in Philadelphia. The speculators, the developers, the shopkeepers, the suburbanites, looking for the latest "in" place to live, should not obscure or overwhelm the people who helped rebuild the community and who still wish to live there.

Seattle preservationists and the city have done a commendable job of attempting to retain Pioneer Square's original residents. The poor, the transients, as well as the long-time residents of this original of American skid rows, continue to live and socialize in the midst of a new wave of visitors and residents who are drawn by the many restoration projects in the area. Instead of living in a slum, the poor are now part of a more diverse and vital community. Both the middle-income and the lower-income citizens are the better for it.

Savannah is consciously trying to retain its checkerboard of racial and economic neighborhood diversity. Through rental subsidies and low-income restoration projects, the larger community is assured of both economic and social stability. And above all, Savannah still looks like Savannah.

Arthur Ziegler, although called the preservation prophet of the poor, is actually the prophet for a new age and new maturity for the entire preservation movement. In badly deteriorated poor neighborhoods, he strives to help present residents restore their houses while encouraging middle-income people to move in. In strongly middle-income preservation areas, he makes sure that a significant number of the poor stay in the community. The speculator is always on notice that the community will never be a ghetto again, either white and rich or black and poor. It is the leavening ingredient of economic and social diversity which can create a restored community that will last.

The Importance of Continuity

A community is started on the way to restoration usually because its residents care very much about its history, its architecture, its neighborhood character. They spend a great amount of time and effort to convince local politicians and other public officials that the community is indeed a good place in which to live and invest. They overcome impossible odds and glacial indifference in order to create a positive image for the community and to improve its economic value.

These people—the original pioneers who were active in the neighborhood associations, the local planning committees, and the dozens of other volunteer organizations—are what give the community its renewed identity and its stability.

But often at Stage Four, the stage of Respectability, rising property prices, and a possibly great influx of new residents and investors, the core of original pioneers may be lost to the community. And if they are lost, either by being "burned out" because of overwork or forced out because of rising rents or rising property taxes, the unique and sustaining spirit of the community may be lost as well.

Too many newcomers to the concept of preservation and to our restoring communities only see the priceless restored architecture, the stained glass, the quaint restaurants and condominiums. They do not see or appreciate the deep foundation of community concern and participation which it takes in order to keep a restored community intact and attractive.

A community of beautiful buildings and charming history is like a glittering antique automobile. It is priceless, a work of art. But if the wrong people get into the driver's seat, people who do not understand the degree of concern and maintenance it needs, that vehicle can soon be a pile of glittering and unworkable junk.

The battle-scarred pioneers know the constant care which a neighborhood needs: hundreds of hours at planning meetings, zoning meetings, city council meetings. There are the constant little concerns of street cleaning, garbage pickup, sign controls, land-use controls, neighborhood communication. The pioneers had to be street people, had to know everyone on the block and in city hall. They understood that "salvation by bricks" will only work if a liberal amount of their own blood, sweat, and tears was used as mortar.

But once the big battle for neighborhood re-newal is over, and a new generation of residents and property owners arrive, what then? Who then will carry on the constant skirmishes to preserve the diversity of the community, the little people and the little "mom and pop" stores every real neighborhood needs? Can a restored community survive on $40,000-a-year residents, and franchised shopping centers, and still keep its historic soul?

After the buildings are saved, save the people who accomplished it. Save a sense of community, a healthy sense of outrage which these original pioneers brought to the neighborhood meetings. Too much development money with too little genuine resident involvement can soon tip the curve from Stage Four Respectability to Stage Five Deterioration. Retaining a few of Stage Two's last angry men and women can help greatly in prolonging a genuine sense of revitalization in a community.

Where Does Preservation End?

Most of the Historic District legislation enacted in our nation is an attempt to save and revive old neighborhoods which are either badly deteriorated or somehow threatened with demolition. But recently some cities are considering the enactment of Conservation Districts which are not badly deteriorated nor presently threatened.

This opens a new era in American preservation which emphasizes the value of the total urban environment, the "less than historic" neighborhoods which are the backbone of a city's life and which maintain the uniqueness of a city. This is almost a form of preventive preservation which assures that a younger neighborhood will be able to reach the age when it too can be called historic.

Neighborhood conservation is preservation in its broadest sense, a concern for a community's total environment of structures and people, giving the community a premeditated assessment of value and providing legislative tools to assure that its integrity will not be destroyed. This enables the building of compatible new construction where applicable as well as encouraging the restoration of older structures.

The city of Portland, Oregon, has nominated two neighborhoods to be Historic Conservation Zones. Ladd's Addition was one of the first West Coast efforts at city planning and Portland's first planned community. Lair Hill was the city's first immigrant community. Although neither is badly deteriorated or has many architectural landmarks, the combination of long-time residents and their old buildings sums up a new dimension in preservation and civic concern.

In order to preserve this unique mixture of architecture and residents, the Portland Historical Landmarks Commission will review all proposed new construction or demolition in the areas. The Conservation Zone designation will strengthen the communities' identity and warn away any developers or city agencies who have intentions to change the character of the neighborhoods.

Even the federal government, once the biggest booster of progress at the price of the past, is beginning to recognize the importance of preservation. To meet the problem of rapidly disappearing engineering and industrial sites, the National Park Service in 1969 established the Historic American Engineering Record. This created

Tourists and long-time residents rest side by side in Seattle's Pioneer Square district. As the area was being restored, preservationists made sure that local services and lodging for low-income residents would remain.

archival documentation of important historic industrial structures, both to encourage their preservation and to provide permanent records of them.

The National Endowment for the Arts, which was allowed in the mid-1960s to include preservation-related endeavors among the activities eligible for funding, has given wise and indispensable assistance to key local preservation organizations. The National Environmental Policy Act of 1969 requires federal agencies to evaluate and disclose project impact upon historical resources as part of their assessment of environmental consequences of federal action. The Emergency Home Purchase Assistance Act of 1974 allows use of low-interest loans to rehabilitate historic structures. The Housing and Community Development Act of 1974 lists historic preservation as one of the activities in which localities may earmark their share of federal community development funds. The Public Buildings Cooperative Use Act of 1976 authorizes the General Services Administration to lease or purchase and rejuvenate buildings of historic or architectural significance and to convert those buildings into federal office space. The Federal Home Mortgage Disclosure Act of 1975 discourages financial institutions from the redlining and withholding of loans from deteriorated communities. In addition, other federal preservation efforts go on through the National Register of Historic Landmarks, the National Trust for Historic Preservation, the National Register of Historic Places, and the Historic American Buildings Survey. Each year, Congress is generating more creative and more far-reaching preservation legislative efforts.

With so much growing governmental interest in historic preservation, with commercial developers and financial institutions beginning to enthusiastically invest in adaptive re-use, with a growing number of communities creating their own neighborhood associations and preservation organizations, there is a greater need than ever to question and encourage every step of this phenomenal advance of American preservation.

Our nation is on the verge of establishing a bold new policy for urban revitalization and the conservation of our resources. The lonely efforts of preservationists in Savannah, St. Paul, Cincin-

The concept of historic and architectural preservation has extended beyond eighteenth- and nineteenth-century mansions. Even such mundane structures as this 1930s filling station in Milwaukee have their preservation adherents who argue for preservation of structures that symbolize significant eras of recent American history.

One of the most difficult, yet absolutely necessary, factors in restoring a community is the sensitive application of new infill construction. This addition to a historically and architecturally important San Francisco bank building shows that new and old architecture can be compatible.

nati, Pittsburgh, Seattle, and many other cities are now beginning to effect the future of all of us. Whether we achieve a long and happy existence at the peak of the preservation bell-curve somewhere between stages Three and Four, or if we allow our communities to settle for Stage Five, depends on us, our personal community involvement, our dedication to the continuing concern for the restoration and preservation of a neighborhood's people as well as its architecture.

Edward Irving Koch, at the beginning of 1978, was inaugurated as the 105th mayor of New York City. He proclaimed, "These have been hard times. We have been tested by fire. We have been drawn across the knife edge of poverty. . . . A better city requires the one ingredient that money cannot buy, people who are willing to give of themselves. . . . As New York in the eighteenth and nineteenth centuries led in the building of urban America, so we must now lead in the rebuilding of America's cities."

The Renegades of Harlem are answering Mayor Koch's call. The Silvermans of San Francisco, the Skolneks of Seattle, the Lyndens of St. Paul, the Forkerts of Chicago, the Willettes of Portland, the Roses of Boston, the Adamses of Savannah, the Dohertys of Galveston, the multitudes of other Americans are also responding to the demands of a new national direction.

The return to the cities, the return to our history, has begun. The people, the old neighborhoods, are now re-creating their own future and in the process are reshaping America.

PART FIVE

Getting Started:
Whom Can You Call for Help

A few years ago, a person who wished to return to the city and restore an old building would probably have been given the advice to have his head examined. Today, there are many avenues of sympathetic assistance for the preservationist.

When considering restoring a structure in any neighborhood, first get to know the people in that neighborhood. Don't be afraid to knock on neighbors' doors and introduce yourself. Watch for someone who may be working on his house. Congratulate him on what a fine job he is doing. You will have a fast friend and a valuable source of information in minutes.

Don't be put off by deterioration or "slum conditions" in the area. Even the most badly deteriorated neighborhood will often have some of the most interesting and likable residents. Find out the real condition of the community from its residents. Has any property changed hands lately? Is there any rehabilitation going on? Are there any community groups meeting? What was the value of local property five years ago, five months ago? Has there been any increase in prices lately? Who is moving in, or out?

Ask local residents for the name of a good realtor to contact. It is important to find a realtor who is familiar with the area because often, if the neighborhood is deteriorated, the majority of realtors may not be familiar with it or may actively try to dissuade you from being interested in it. Let the local realtor show you around. He may not understand why you wish to actually restore an old building, but he will give you an idea of what is on the market and what the prevailing prices are.

Then once you are able to familiarize yourself with the area, once you get the feel for the people and the structures, you should be able to at least know if you want to be a part of the community. If you are still interested and if you have decided on a building you wish to purchase, then it is time to begin a more intensive investigation by talking with:

1. The local neighborhood association—Every community usually has some kind of neighborhood organization. An offshoot of the old Model Cities organization, a commercial association, a church social group, or a neighborhood association can bring you in contact with the residents who are most active and usually most concerned about the betterment of the community. Ask them about area schools and what is being done to improve them. Also, ask the names of reliable local contractors who could look at the property you are interested in to check for structural defects and to give cost estimates for the rehabilitation work you won't be able to do. If the area has

an active neighborhood improvement association, then you know that this community is on the way to restoring itself.

2. A city-wide preservation organization—Even if there is no neighborhood association, there may be an organization which is concerned about city-wide preservation. This group may not only be able to help your restoration project but may also help you start a local neighborhood association. The private, nonprofit organization can often be the most effective action group of all.

3. The local city planning agency—It seems that the one city agency usually most sensitive to preservation and most knowledgeable about the deteriorated neighborhoods is the city planning department. Call and ask to talk with someone involved in historic preservation. You should be able to find at least one invaluable friend who may be able to tell you more about your particular neighborhood and also tell you about building permits, zoning, financing, et cetera.

4. The local historical society—The local historical society may or may not be of help. Unfortunately, some societies still see themselves as the depository of old photos and records of buildings which have already been torn down, and not as action organizations which try to preserve the historic community. But some societies, especially the state societies, are now very actively involved in preservation as well as documentation. Call them and ask for help, both for information about the historicity of the building you are interested in and for help regarding the preservation of it.

5. The local bank—Your local banker also may or may not be helpful in securing financing for your restoration venture. But he should be at least a source of information regarding the community and its possible economic health. If your local financial institutions are not helpful, even after your supplying them with the Ideal Loan Application, see the next step.

6. The local Neighborhood Housing Services Program—This program, which grew out of the neighborhood preservation activities in Pittsburgh, is now operating in about fifty cities across the nation. If your community doesn't have a branch of the NHS, contact the Urban Reinvestment Task Force, 1120–19th Street, N.W., Washington, D.C. 20036, or phone 202/634–1689.

The Task Force assists in the creation of an operating program for an NHS community organization, which includes a private, state-chartered corporation with a 501 (c)(3) tax-exempt status. The corporation is governed by a local board of directors, which includes neighborhood residents, at-large community members, financial institution representatives, and city government people. From an office in the neighborhood, a small staff provides the following services:

* Rehabilitation counseling—an analysis of home-repair needs, work write-ups, cost estimates, and home-repair counseling.

* Construction monitoring services—on-site inspections and co-ordination with contractors and residents.

* Financial services—financial counseling to residents, prepurchase counseling and arranging financing for mortgages, and solving real estate problems hindering property improvement.

Help from National Organizations

There are other national organizations which may be able to help you as an individual preservationist or as a community organization. One of the key national preservation organizations is the National Trust for Historic Preservation. It is a private, nonprofit corporation chartered by Congress to facilitate public participation in the preservation of historic properties. The Trust owns and maintains certain historic properties of national significance and assists public and private agencies and individuals in historic preservation.

A wide variety of educational and technical assistance activities are provided by the Trust, including publications, professional and technical seminars and conferences, matching consultant services grants, legal services, preparation of feasibility studies, acceptance of preservation easements, and the purchase of options on endangered historic properties. For more information, contact: Field Services Division, National Trust for Historic Preservation, 740 Jackson Place, N.W., Washington, D.C. 20006.

' The National Register has been a major tool for the preservation of historic structures since the Tax Reform Act of 1976 provided tax incentives for the preservation of structures on the National Register. The Register is the official inventory of the nation's properties that merit preservation because of their significance in American history, architecture, archaeology, and culture. The National Register includes all historic areas in the National Park System, all properties designated by the Secretary of the Interior as National Historic Landmarks, and other properties of national, state, and local significance. Districts, sites, buildings, structures, and objects may be nominated by the State Historic Preservation Officer following the recommendations of a State historic preservation review board and, upon approval by the National Park Service, are listed in the National Register. For more information about how you and your community may benefit from National Register designation, contact: Director, National Park Service, U. S. Department of the Interior, Washington, D.C. 20240.

Other national preservation organizations include:

Advisory Council on Historic Preservation
Suite 530
1522 K Street, N.W.
Washington, D.C. 20005

American Institute of Architects
Committee on Historic Resources
1735 New York Avenue, N.W.
Washington, D.C. 20006

Don't Tear It Down
Box 14043, Ben Franklin Station
Washington, D.C. 20004

Preservation Action
2101 L Street, N.W.
Suite 906
Washington, D.C. 20037

General Services Administration
Historic Preservation Program
18th and F Streets, N.W.
Washington, D.C. 20405

National Endowment for the Arts
Architecture and Environmental Arts
Washington, D.C. 20506

Society for Architectural Historians
Room 716
1700 Walnut Street
Philadelphia, Pennsylvania 10103

Society for Industrial Archeology
Suite 5020
National Museum of History and Technology
Smithsonian Institution
Washington, D.C. 20560

Preservation Publications

Fortunately for the preservation do-it-yourselfer, there are many good publications which can help you do everything from fixing up an old house to organizing a neighborhood preservation action group.

One of the most interesting publications is a monthly magazine called *The Old House Journal.* Written by and for people who are involved in all the details of restoring an old house, the magazine gives a great deal of encouragement and specific help to the person struggling with old floors, plumbing, light fixtures, and wallpaper stripping.

Clem Labine, editor of *The Old House Journal,* will send a sample copy of his national publication if you write to: *The Old House Journal,* 199 Berkeley Place, Brooklyn, New York 11217. He also answers subscribers' renovation questions.

American Preservation is a slick, mass appeal bimonthly magazine which highlights attractive preservation areas around the nation as well as providing news and comments on historic and neighborhood preservation. Published by *American Preservation,* Bracy House, 620 East Sixth, Little Rock, Arkansas 72202.

Preservation Briefs is provided by the National Technical Information Service and the Office of Archeology and Historic Preservation. They are a series of very helpful technical manuals on different aspects of restoration and adaptive re-use of old buildings. The issues include: "The Cleaning and Waterproof Coating of Masonry Buildings" and "Repointing Mortar Joints in Historic Brick Buildings."

In addition, the agencies offer reading lists of other publications on subjects such as adaptive use of historic buildings, stone preservation, and wood deterioration and preservation. Addresses are: Office of Archeology and Historic Preservation, National Park Service, U. S. Department of the Interior, Washington, D.C. 20240 or National Technical Service, Department of Commerce, 5285 Port Royal Road, Springfield, Virginia 22161.

The Old House Catalog is a book by Lawrence Grow which has listings and comments about 2,500 products, including rare old-house items and hard-to-find craftspeople. It also offers advice on furnishing and decorating the period home. Published by Main Street/Universe Books, 381 Park Avenue South, New York, N.Y. 10016.

The Old House Journal Buyers' Guide is edited by the Old House Journal's editorial staff. This book lists many restorer's buying sources. Can be ordered from Universe Books, 381 Park Avenue, South, New York, N.Y. 10016.

Preservation Press of the National Trust has been publishing many books which will be helpful to the preservationist. Here are just a few:

A Guide to State Historic Preservation Programs, by Betts Able. A directory of state programs, enabling legislation, publications, National Park Service grant-in-air projects, and state historic preservation offices.

Economic Benefits of Preserving Old Buildings is a helpful compilation of papers on criteria and legal and financial techniques for the adaptive use of old buildings, including case studies.

A Guide to Federal Programs: Programs and Activities Related to Historic Preservation, by Nancy D. Schultz. Information on two hundred programs and activities, including descriptions, criteria for participation, program examples, and offices to contact. Also, a new 1976 Supplement of the book is now available.

In addition, by becoming a member of the National Trust, you receive the monthly *Preservation News.* It is a timely news magazine about preservation legislation, programs, and preservation opinion and commentary. In addition, a new newsletter for neighborhood groups called *Conserve Neighborhoods* is being published by the Trust's Neighborhood Conservation Information Service. For complete information, contact: The National Trust, 740 Jackson Place, N.W., Washington, D.C. 20006.

Historic Preservation in Inner City Areas: A Manual of Practice is written by Pittsburgh preservationist Arthur P. Ziegler, Jr. A fine guide for preservationists telling how to organize preservation programs in urban neighborhoods, giving details on funding and publicity. Published by the Allegheney Press, Pittsburgh.

Revolving Funds for Historic Preservation: A Manual of Practice was written by Arthur Ziegler, Jr., Leopold Adler II, and Walter C. Kidney. A very good explanation of how preservationists can use the revolving fund for financing the rehabilitation of a deteriorating community. Published by Ober Park Associates, Inc., Pittsburgh.

The Death and Life of Great American Cities, by Jane Jacobs. This is probably the one book which has done more for the back-to-the-city movement than any other. Jacobs was one of the first voices to effectively speak out against urban renewal and to define the real values of urban life and architecture. An eloquent book that has helped shape the thinking of most urban preservationists. Published by Vintage Books.

There are many other books and publications which are being directed to the growing preservation movement. This proliferation of publications is in itself an indication that the return-to-the-city and stay-in-the-city preservation movement is becoming a major national growth industry.

How to Restore a Building

The basic question for preservationists is "What is a 'restored' historic building?" This question is especially critical now that the Tax Reform Act of 1976 provides deductions to property owners for structures cited by the Secretary of the Interior as "Certified Rehabilitations." In addition, National Register designation makes homeowners eligible for Title I Home Improvement Loans and can provide preservation funding for other projects through the block-grant program of the Housing and Community Development Act of 1974.

The property owner must obtain application for certification, preferably before work begins, and request an inspection of the work. Under proposed regulations issued by the Department of the Interior (Federal Register, March 15, 1977, 36 CFR Part 76), the work is to be reviewed by the State Historic Preservation Officer and a representative of the Secretary of the Interior and evaluated in terms of consistency with the Standards of Rehabilitation.

The check list which follows has been developed by the Department of the Interior to define what constitutes a restoration process which could be considered "Certified Rehabilitation." Of course, the structure must meet the other criteria regarding historical importance, et cetera, as outlined in the earlier chapter titled "How to Gain Control . . ." But even if you don't wish to place your building on the National Register, these guidelines are still a good way to help you do a better job of truly "restoring" your property instead of merely "fixing it up." True restoration will give you greater aesthetic satisfaction and greater property value as well.

STANDARDS OF REHABILITATION CHECK LIST

The Environment

Consider:	Avoid:
Retaining distinctive features such as the size, scale, mass, color, and materials of buildings, including roofs, porches, and stairways that give a neighborhood its distinguishing character.	Introducing new construction into neighborhoods which is incompatible with the character of the district because of size, scale, color, and materials.

Consider:

Using new plant materials, fencing, walkways, and street furniture which are compatible with the character of the neighborhood in size, scale, material, and color.

Retaining landscape features such as parks, gardens, street furniture, walkways, streets, alleys, and building setbacks which have traditionally linked buildings to their environment.

Avoid:

Introducing signs, street lighting, street furniture, new plant materials, fencing, walkways, and paving materials which are out of scale or inappropriate to the neighborhood.

Destroying the relationship of buildings and their environment by widening existing streets, changing paving material, or by introducing poorly designed and poorly located new streets and parking lots or introducing new construction incompatible with the character of the neighborhood.

Building: Lot

Consider:

Inspecting the lot carefully to locate and identify plants, trees, fencing, walkways, and street furniture which might be an important part of the property's history and development.

Retaining plants, trees, fencing, walkways, and street furniture which reflect the property's history and development.

Basing all decisions of new work on actual knowledge of the past appearance of the property found in photographs, drawings, newspapers, and tax records. If changes are made, they should be carefully evaluated in light of the past appearance of the site.

Avoid:

Making hasty changes to the appearance of the site by removing old plants, trees, fencing, walkways, and street furniture before evaluating their importance in the property's history and development.

Overrestoring the site to an appearance it never had.

Buildings: Exterior Features
(*Masonry Buildings*)

Consider:

Retaining original masonry and mortar, whenever possible, without the application of any surface treatment.

Duplicating old mortar in composition, color, and textures.

Duplicating old mortar in joint size, method of application, and joint profile.

Repairing stucco with a stucco mixture duplicating the original as closely as possible in appearance and texture.

Avoid:

Applying waterproof or water-repellent coatings or other treatments unless required to solve a specific technical problem that has been studied and identified. Coatings are frequently unnecessary, expensive, and can accelerate deterioration of the masonry.

Repointing with mortar of high Portland cement content can create a bond that is often stronger than the building material. This can cause deterioration as a result of the differing coefficient of expansion and the differing porosity of the material and the mortar.

Consider:	**Avoid:**
Cleaning masonry only when necessary to halt deterioration and always with the gentlest method possible, such as low-pressure water and soft, natural-bristle brushes.	Repointing with mortar joints of a differing size or joint profile, texture, or color.
	Sandblasting brick or stone surfaces: this method of cleaning erodes the surface of the material and accelerates deterioration.
Repairing or replacing, where necessary, deteriorated material with new material that duplicates the old as closely as possible.	Using chemical cleaning products which could have an adverse chemical reaction with the masonry materials, i.e., acid on limestone or marble.
Replacing missing architectural features, such as cornices, brackets, railings, and shutters.	Applying new material which is inappropriate or was unavailable when the building was constructed, such as artificial brick siding, artificial cast stone or brick veneer.
Retaining the original or early color and texture of masonry surfaces, wherever possible. Brick or stone surfaces may have been painted or whitewashed for practical and aesthetic reasons.	Removing architectural features, such as cornices, brackets, shutters, window architraves, and doorway pediments. These are usually an essential part of a building's character and appearance, illustrating the continuity of growth and change.
	Indiscriminate removal of paint from masonry surfaces. This may be historically incorrect and may also subject the building to harmful damage.

Frame Buildings

Consider:	**Avoid:**
Retaining original material, whenever possible.	Removing architectural features such as siding, cornices, brackets, window architraves, and doorway pediments. These are in most cases essential parts of a building's character and appearance, illustrating the continuity of growth and change.
Repairing or replacing, where necessary, deteriorated material that duplicates the old as closely as possible.	Resurfacing frame buildings with new material which is inappropriate, or was unavailable when the building was constructed, such as artificial stone, brick veneer, asbestos or asphalt shingles, plastic or aluminum siding. Such material also can contribute to the deterioration of the structure from moisture and insect attack.

Roofs

Consider:	**Avoid:**
Preserving the original roof shape.	Changing the original roof shape or adding features inappropriate to the essential character of

Consider:	**Avoid:**
Retaining the original roofing material, whenever possible.	the roof such as oversized dormer windows or picture windows.
Replacing deteriorated roof coverings with new material that matches the old in composition, size, shape, color, and texture.	Applying new roofing material that is inappropriate to the style and period of the building and the neighborhood.
Preserving or replacing, where necessary, all architectural features which give the roof its essential character, such as dormer windows, cupolas, cornices, brackets, chimneys, cresting, and weather vanes.	Replacing deteriorated roof coverings with new materials which differ to such an extent from the old in composition, size, shape, color, and texture that the appearance of the building is altered.
Placing television antennae and mechanical equipment, such as air conditioners, in an inconspicuous location.	Stripping the roof of architectural features important to its character.
	Placing television antennae and mechanical equipment, such as air conditioners, where they can be seen from the street.

Windows and Doors

Consider:	**Avoid:**
Retaining existing window and door openings, including window sash, glass, lintels, sills, architraves, shutters, doors, pediments, hoods, steps, and all hardware.	Introducing new window and door openings into the principal elevations, or enlarging or reducing window or door openings to fit new stock window sash or new stock door sizes.
Respecting the stylistic period or periods a building represents. If replacement of window sashes or doors is necessary, the replacement should duplicate the material, design, and the hardware of the older window sash or door.	Altering the size of window panes or sashes. Such changes destroy the scale and proportion of the building.
	Discarding original doors and door hardware when they can be repaired and reused in place.
	Inappropriate new window or door features such as aluminum storm and screen window combinations that require the removal of original windows and doors or the installation of plastic or metal strip awnings or fake shutters that disturb the character and appearance of the building.

Porches and Steps

Consider:	**Avoid:**
Retaining porches and steps which are appropriate to the building and its development. Porches or additions reflecting later architectural styles are often important to the building's historical integrity and, whenever possible, should be retained.	Removing or altering porches and steps which are appropriate to the building and its development and the style it represents.
	Stripping porches and steps of original material and architectural features, such as handrails,

Consider:	**Avoid:**
Repairing or replacing, where necessary, deteriorated architectural features of wood, iron, cast iron, terra-cotta, tile, and brick.	balusters, columns, brackets, and roof decoration of wood, iron, cast iron, terra cotta, tile, and brick.
Repairing or replacing, where necessary, deteriorated material with new material that duplicates the old as closely as possible.	Applying new material which is inappropriate or was unavailable when the building was constructed, such as artificial cast stone, brick veneer, asbestos or asphalt shingles, or plastic or aluminum siding.
	Enclosing porches and steps in a manner that destroys their intended appearance.

Buildings: Exterior Finishes

Consider:	**Avoid:**
Discovering and retaining original paint colors, or repainting with colors based on the original to illustrate the distinctive character of the property.	Repainting with colors that cannot be documented through research and investigation to be appropriate to the building and neighborhood.

Buildings: Interior Features

Consider:	**Avoid:**
Retaining original material, architectural features, and hardware, whenever possible, such as stairs, handrails, balusters, mantelpieces, cornices, chair rails, baseboards, paneling, doors and doorways, wallpaper, lighting fixtures, locks, and doorknobs.	Removing original material, architectural features, and hardware except where essential for safety or efficiency.
Repairing or replacing, where necessary, deteriorated material with new material that duplicates the old as closely as possible.	Installing new decorative material which is inappropriate or was unavailable when the building was constructed, such as vinyl-plastic or imitation-wood wall and floor coverings except in utility areas such as kitchens and bathrooms.
Retaining original plaster, whenever possible.	Destroying original plaster except where necessary for safety and efficiency.
Discovering and retaining original paint colors, wallpapers, and other decorative motifs or, where necessary, replacing them with colors, wallpapers, or decorative motifs based on the original.	

Plan and Function

Consider:	**Avoid:**
Using a building for its intended purposes.	Altering a building to accommodate an incompatible use requiring extensive alterations to the plan, materials, and appearance of the building.
Finding an adaptive use, when necessary, which is compatible with the plan, structure, and appearance of the building.	

Consider:	**Avoid:**
Retaining the basic plan of a building, whenever possible.	Altering the basic plan of a building by demolishing principal walls, partitions, and stairways.

New Additions

Consider:	**Avoid:**
Keeping new additions to a minimum and making them compatible in scale, building materials, and texture.	Making unnecessary new additions.
Designing new additions to be compatible in materials, size, scale, color, and texture with the earlier building and the neighborhood.	Designing new additions which are incompatible with the earlier building and the neighborhood in materials, size, scale, and texture.
Using contemporary designs compatible with the character and mood of the building or the neighborhood.	Imitating an earlier style or period of architecture in new additions, except in rare cases where a contemporary design would detract from the architectural unity of an ensemble or group. Especially avoid imitating an earlier style of architecture in new additions that have a completely contemporary function such as a drive-in bank or garage.

Mechanical Services: Heating, Electrical, and Plumbing

Consider:	**Avoid:**
Installing necessary building services in areas and spaces that will require the least possible alteration to the plan, materials, and appearance of the building.	Causing unnecessary damage to the plan, materials, and appearance of the building when installing mechanical services.
Installing the vertical runs of ducts, pipes, and cables in closets, service rooms, and wall cavities.	Installing vertical runs of ducts, pipes, and cables in places where they will be a visual intrusion.
Selecting mechanical systems that best suit the building.	Cutting holes in important architectural features, such as cornices, decorative ceilings, and paneling.
Rewiring early lighting fixtures.	Installing "dropped" acoustical ceilings to hide inappropriate mechanical systems. This destroys the proportions and character of the room.
Having exterior electrical and telephone cables installed underground.	Having exterior electrical and telephone cables attached to the principal elevations of the buildings.

Safety and Code Requirements

Consider:
Complying with code requirements in such a manner that the essential character of a building is preserved intact.

Consider:

Investigating variances for historic properties afforded under some local codes.

Installing adequate fire-prevention equipment in a manner which does minimal damage to the appearance or fabric of a property.

Providing access for the handicapped without damaging the essential character of a property.

This restoration check list goes far beyond what most people consider "rehabilitation." It helps define what this book is all about—the sensitive use of an old building which respects its surrounding neighborhood, its history, and its architecture. Whether a person is restoring a historic home or adapting the use of an old commercial structure, these guidelines can still make good design and economic sense to the developer.

Sensitivity, concern for our neighbors, a compassionate understanding of history and its architecture—this is what makes a well-restored building, a happy neighborhood, a wise person. It is really what historic preservation is all about and why people are returning to the city. It is the grass-roots process of building a better future from the worthy remnants of our past.

Preservation can be enjoyable. It can be profitable for all of us, rich and poor alike. And it can be an activity so fulfilling that it has to be experienced to be believed. So the next time you drive through a deteriorated urban area, look up, look around. You may discover beauty, and a new kind of commitment, in the most unexpected places.